The Golden Voice of the Senate

The Golden Voice o

he Senate By Annette Culler Penney

Foreword by Senator Mike Mansfield

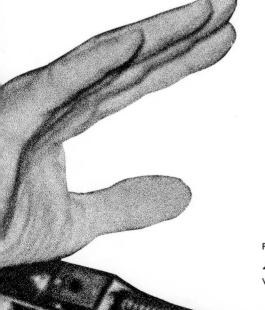

PUBLISHED BY

Acropolis Books

WASHINGTON, D. C. 20009

AMERICANA
ACROPOLIS

THE CONGRESSIONAL LEADERSHIP SERIES

Volume No. 1
HOW A SENATOR MAKES GOVERNMENT WORK
METCALF OF MONTANA
by Richard D. Warden

Volume No. 2
LIBERAL LEADER IN THE HOUSE
FRANK THOMPSON, JR.
by Augusta Elliott Wilson

Volume No. 3
THE GOLDEN VOICE OF THE SENATE
DIRKSEN OF ILLINOIS
by Annette Culler Penney

ACROPOLIS BOOKS
Colortone Building, 2400 17th St., N.W.
Washington, D. C. 20009

CONGRESSIONAL LEADERSHIP SERIES • VOLUME NO. 3

Printed in the United States of America by
Colortone Creative Printing
Washington, D. C. 20009

Type set in Baskerville
by Colortone Typographic Division, Inc.

Design by Design and Art Studio 2400, Inc.

Library of Congress Catalog Number 68-56200

CONTENTS

A MOVING LINCOLN DAY SPEECH IS DELIVERED BY
SENATOR DIRKSEN AT THE LINCOLN MEMORIAL
IN WASHINGTON, D. C. SENATOR THRUSTON B.
MORTON, KENTUCKY, LISTENS MOST ATTENTIVELY.

FOREWORD

Senator Everett McKinley Dirksen and I see a great deal of each other. We meet frequently to discuss the legislative program and other business of the Senate. As Majority and Minority Leaders, we are political opponents even as we are personal friends and Senate collaborators. Almost as though to seal this relationship, we shake hands across the center aisle of the Senate Chamber at the opening of each session. The daily handshake is a reminder to me of the great strength Everett McKinley Dirksen contributes to his State, the Senate, and the Nation.

It is appropriate that this book is called "The Golden Voice of the Senate." The voice of Senator Dirksen is, indeed, rich and colorful, as any one of the thousands who have listened to him from the galleries of the Senate will attest. His speeches are filled with an eloquent idiom and delightful humor which mark him as one of the nation's outstanding orators. The oratory, however, is far more than sound deep. It is sustained by a rich and rounded personality. Senator Dirksen brings to his key role in the Senate a native wisdom, a thoughtful scholarship, an active intelligence and an immense human experience. His roots are in the Midwest; yet his stature, as dedicated leader, is that of a man for all parts of America. Everett McKinley Dirksen is as Republican as his middle name. Beyond all else, however, he is an outstanding Senator and a distinguished American patriot.

MIKE MANSFIELD
U. S. Senator from Montana
Senate Majority Leader

THE UNITED STATES SENATE

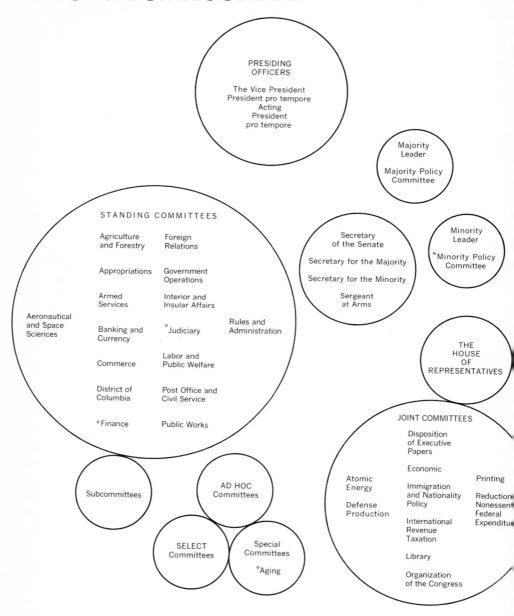

PRESIDING
OFFICERS

The Vice President
President pro tempore
Acting
President
pro tempore

Majority
Leader

Majority Policy
Committee

STANDING COMMITTEES

Agriculture
and Forestry

Foreign
Relations

Appropriations

Government
Operations

Armed
Services

Interior and
Insular Affairs

Aeronautical
and Space
Sciences

Banking and
Currency

*Judiciary

Rules and
Administration

Commerce

Labor and
Public Welfare

District of
Columbia

Post Office and
Civil Service

*Finance

Public Works

Secretary
of the Senate

Secretary for the Majority

Secretary for the Minority

Sergeant
at Arms

Minority
Leader

*Minority Policy
Committee

THE
HOUSE
OF
REPRESENTATIVES

JOINT COMMITTEES

Disposition
of Executive
Papers

Economic

Atomic
Energy

Immigration
and Nationality
Policy

Printing

Defense
Production

International
Revenue
Taxation

Reduction
Nonessent
Federal
Expenditu

Library

Organization
of the Congress

Subcommittees

AD HOC
Committees

SELECT
Committees

Special
Committees

*Aging

*Office and Committee Assignments, Senator Everett McKinley Dirksen.

In addition he serves on the
following commissions in the 90th Congress:

- The Select Commission on Western Hemisphere Immigration
- The Senate Office Building Commission
- The Commission for the Extension of the U. S. Capitol

THE SENATE MINORITY LEADER must be the guiding spirit in all legislative and political matters facing members of the Senate; he must direct as well as persuade the members of his party in the United States Senate to follow, or at least consider in a favorable light, legislation pending.

The man holding this post must be a leader in all things relating to the business of the United States Senate and of his party group which has the fewest number in that part of Congress. While leading the minority in legislative combat against their opponents across the aisle, he also maintains, with wisdom born out of experience, a practical cooperation with the majority leader. First, in his thinking, is the nation's best interest.

Not least important, he acts as the principal spokesman for the minority of the Senate directly to the American people in order that they may more clearly understand all aspects of every issue, and thereby exercise their own roles as citizens most effectively.

THE WITTY SENATOR DIRKSEN has been a favorite subject for most Washington reporters during his entire career in the United States Congress. Whether they praised or panned him, at least he always provided writers with plenty of ammunition as well as erudite quotes, which frequently made the front page.

We avid Dirksen fans always felt that the news gatherers who panned the master of metaphor suffered from deep seated envy or from a similar psychotic malady.

Having been a Dirksen observer for many years and a collector of fun stories about him, I have always delighted in his well-placed thrusts at his adversaries and his ability to remain on the top of the political heep.

These are just a few of the reasons why I wanted to write this book and preserve for posterity the highlights of the career of this political phenomenon.

A. C. P.

THE HAPPY SMILES OF TWO TOP REPUBLICANS,
SENATORS DIRKSEN AND CHARLES H. PERCY,
MIGHT HAVE SOMETHING TO DO WITH THEIR HAV-
ING THEIR PICTURE MADE WITH THE MOST FAMED
OF ALL REPUBLICANS, ANOTHER ILLINOIS FAVOR-
ITE, ABRAHAM LINCOLN.

1

A SENATOR'S SENATOR

■ Great men of Congress of these United States have come and gone since the handful of American patriots met in Philadelphia to carve the stepping stones that led this nation to greatness. But only a few have made their mark distinctly, clearly and with a majesty that vibrates patriotism and statesmanship.

It is not unlikely that the name Everett McKinley Dirksen will glitter brightly on the marquee of Congressional history when the list is mounted and a review made of major accomplishments. Also, it is not unlikely that he will be known as one of the few who basked throughout his career in the heady glow of tribute from Presidents, fellow Senators and Congressmen from both ends of the political spectrum, and—above all—from the hard-to-impress Washington press corps.

He has been praised as one of the greatest statesmen of this century by many of his colleagues and from political writers who have followed his career with mounting interest.

His stance has always been based on what he felt could best benefit the country in a given set of circumstances and in the mercurial international climate. He, more than many younger Congressional colleagues, realizes that situations do not remain static and so decries the short-sightedness of those who believe tomorrow's problems will be comfortably cloaked in today's answers. He often quotes Victor Hugo in clarifying his position on issues: ''No army can with-

A QUIET MOMENT WITH SENATOR MARGARET CHASE SMITH, MAINE, ALLOWS DIRKSEN TO GET DOWN TO CASES IN QUIET DISCUSSION ON LEGISLATIVE MATTERS.

stand the strength of an idea whose time has come."
Thus, he proceeds to follow this line of thinking while
bearing in mind the long-range view. It is this blend
of legislative insight plus his willingness to listen to
another's point of view and his incomparable ability
to affect harmony among dissident Congressional members that have made him a valuable leader.

A prime responsibility of a Majority or Minority
Leader of either House of Congress is to keep peace
and harmony among party members so as to maintain
an effective bloc of strength from which to operate in
the face of antagonistic opposition. It is vital to be able
to blend the best ideas of each side and to work out a
solution so the most constructive legislation may be
effected.

To Senator Everett McKinley Dirksen this was a
singular and awesome challenge, particularly since he
knew some of his Republican colleagues had wanted
a more liberal personage as the Senate Minority Leader.
Also, there had been no real strong leadership for years
in this particular capacity, though the leaders who
preceded him were highly capable and devoted Americans. To make his job even more difficult, he was
facing the Senate when he became leader in 1959
with less than a one-third Republican minority. By the
Ninetieth Congress (1967-1968), his situation had im-
proved appreciably, as he had thirty-six Republican
Senators—all highly capable, individualistic and hard

working men. By that time Dirksen had long been noted as having done more to unify the Republicans than any other leader before him in this century.

No-one could have more succinctly described the feelings of the minority group about their leader than did one of the noted liberals of the Republican Party, Senator Jacob Javits, when he commented: "I have occasion to oppose his views and he to oppose mine with vigor. But, I like him. He can be amenable. He knows how to develop an amalgam of views among thirty-two other high-powered prima donnas on the Republican side. Yet he can be very stubborn, and we hope we don't run into the blunt end of his stubbornness. The best posture with him is always to come clean, to deal with him, because that is the way he responds most. He's a very decent, kind, considerate human being and we're all very fond of him."

Being fond of him is one thing, but knowing the full tilt of his power has evoked some jealousy, particularly among the young progressive Senate bucks who have attempted from time to time to test the old master's effectiveness and have come out on the minus side of the ledger. He has been called the most powerful power broker in the country because of his ability to negotiate. He is unlike most of his predecessors who generally held the philosophy that Republicans should vote against everything the Democrats wanted. But his ability to negotiate with both factions has brought

A SENATOR'S SENATOR

SENATOR DIRKSEN APPEARS TO BE GETTING A STRONG VOTE OF CONFIDENCE FROM THE REPUBLICAN POLICY GROUP. FROM LEFT TO RIGHT: SENATORS MARK O. HATFIELD, OREGON; EDWARD W. BROOKE, MASSACHUSETTS; CHARLES H. PERCY, ILLINOIS; CLIFFORD P. HANSEN, WYOMING; HOWARD H. BAKER, JR., TENNESSEE.

much greater strength to the Republican side than has been enjoyed for many years.

It is generally conceded that Dirksen has always been able to do more with his thirty-two to thirty-six Republicans than the former Senator William F. Knowland (R. Calif.) could with his forty-seven during his term as Minority Leader when a Republican President—Eisenhower—was in the White House. It need not be interpreted here that Knowland was any less dedicated a Senator, but he, like those before him, could not match the quality of leadership which Senator Dirksen has exhibited.

Dirksen's logic is compromise, and he is a thoroughly realistic political leader. He has the enviable faculty of appearing to cooperate with the opposition while at the same time using his ability to create a diversion among the opposition ranks. Perhaps his most vital contribution to the GOP leadership has been to maintain pleasant and warm relationships with fellow Republican Senators whose political philosophies vary broadly from his. He does not demand there be a firm stand among all members on a particular issue, nor does he use bulldozer tactics, but he soothes as much as he can with kindness, understanding and, as he has often said: ". . . with the old oil can—it is mightier than the sword."

His efforts in this direction and his willingness to bend a little in a cooperative spirit with the opposite

THE SENATE'S GOLDEN VOICE TAKES A BACK SEAT
TO HIS YOUNG SON-IN-LAW, SENATOR HOWARD H.
BAKER, JR. OF TENNESSEE, WHO APPEARS TO BE
HOLDING HIS OWN WITH WITTY WORDS; MAYBE
UPPING THE NOTED DIRKSEN IN VERBAL QUIPS.
THE AMUSED SENATOR EDWARD W. BROOKE,
MASSACHUSETTS, LOOKS ON APPROVINGLY.

party has kept the Democrats from using their large majority literally to block or destroy everything the Republicans would like to gain. It keeps the Republicans from getting caught napping when important decisions or bills are in the making. In fact, it is widely accepted that Senator Dirksen has enjoyed a large measure of the confidence of the last five Presidents and is thus able to glean worthwhile information with which to forearm the Republicans in Congress. He is able to grasp many gems of ideas for developing his important thrusts for the partisan warfare which shakes the Democrats and solidifies the Republicans on issues.

His hot line to the White House and to influential behind-the-scenes business, labor and international personalities is well known. He stirs attention wherever he goes just by being himself, and the people love it.

Whenever he opens his mouth on the Senate floor, at his weekly press conferences, or before a banquet audience he is automatically quoted around the world. He is a veteran scene stealer, which has helped him to beat the Democrats in the heavily Democratic state of Illinois.

One of the best scenes he ever stole was in July, 1964 when he followed Governor William Scranton of Pennsylvania, who was informing convention delegates about his qualifications to be the party's candidate for the Presidency—a most unfortunate position for anyone, especially without Dirksen's endorsement. The

SENATOR DIRKSEN FREQUENTLY GETS TOGETHER
WITH HOUSE MINORITY LEADER GERALD FORD,
MICHIGAN, TO WORK OUT DETAILS ON THEIR AP-
PROACH TO LEGISLATION.

Senator was endorsing Barry Goldwater for that spot. He explained the reason for some of Goldwater's voting patterns and noted that his vote against cloture on the Senate civil rights filibuster was justified insofar as that Senator was concerned. "You must remember," Senator Dirksen stated in his most magnificent oratorical style, "a vote on cloture is merely a procedural matter. My own disposition generally is against cloture in the Senate. Why, my goodness, Arizona Senators traditionally vote against cloture. I once asked my esteemed colleague, Carl Hayden, the President Pro Tempore of the Senate, about this. He said that if cloture had been invoked on the issue of admitting New Mexico to the Union, Arizona never would have entered the Union. The reason: it was proposed that New Mexico be admitted to the Union with Arizona included within its boundaries. Had that happened, there would be no Arizona today," Senator Dirksen commented in his soothing manner. "I urged Senator Goldwater several times to vote for the bill. But he had reservations on two titles of the bill—the fair employment and accommodations sections. I was well aware of this, but you know it is not my business to quarrel with my fellow Senators. They have convictions. I wouldn't think much of a fellow who didn't have convictions and who didn't assert them."

In nominating Goldwater, he alienated some of the so-called power boys, but this was nothing new in his

A SENATOR'S
SENATOR

SENATOR HIRAM FONG, HAWAII, STOPS BY A BAN-
QUET TABLE TO TALK WITH DIRKSEN AND THE
LATE STYLES BRIDGES. THIS PICTURE WAS MADE
NOT LONG AFTER SENATOR DIRKSEN ARRIVED IN
THE SENATE.

political life. He had been, for years, out of the good graces of Tom Dewey, whom he supported in his abortive attempts to become President, but went against him in 1952.

His political path has not been an easy one, and his love of America and its old fashioned virtues often puts him out of kilter with the progressives, but then he has managed to steer a steady course and come out far better than any of his detractors. "He will be remembered—they will not," is the saying of the Dirksenphiles.

Dirksen's ability to swing Democrats into the Republican camp caused one important Republican Senator to note: "If there are forty-one Republicans in the Senate, Dirksen's power is absolute. At thirty-seven, that power is enormous; at thirty-four, unstable." But another pointed out, "We are well aware we are led by a fighting master of political legislation whose persuasive powers are gently applied at the proper time. If he is so inclined, his opposition to a bill can be a kiss of death."

A grudgingly admiring Democratic Senator told a reporter once: "I'm not getting any younger and I sometimes wonder what my grandchildren will say to their friends about their grandfather's work in the Senate. I think Everett's reached that stage. He's got no more political worlds to conquer. He's felt the winds of mortality. I think he doesn't want to be

A SENATOR'S
SENATOR

SENATOR MILTON R. YOUNG, NORTH DAKOTA,
SHARES A LIGHT MOMENT WITH SENATOR GEORGE
MURPHY, CALIFORNIA, AND SENATOR DIRKSEN.

remembered as the man who played politics while the world burned. He knows the big issues and he's got his conscience working on them. Of course, he's a wise old rat and he can still take you through a lot of back alleys before you find yourself where his conscience wants you.''

His conscience is backed up by his ability to absorb and retain information. He continually studies huge assortments of materials to acquaint himself with every aspect of the bills to come before the Senate as well as to refresh his mind on historical, philosophical and Biblical facts.

One only has to read the *Congressional Record* to see what members of Congress think about Senator Dirksen. The warm regard in which he appears to be held was expressed by Senator Mike Mansfield and many others on the day in May, 1966 when Dirksen broke his hip:

''Mr. President, last night the distinguished Minority Leader entered Walter Reed Hospital for the physical checkup which he undergoes periodically. During the early morning hours, while leaving his bed, Senator Dirksen fell and broke his hip.

''This morning, he is to undergo surgery to reduce and set the fracture.

''We tend to take for granted the presence in this Chamber of the gracious Minority Leader. His stamina, his voice, his manner, his charming uniqueness have

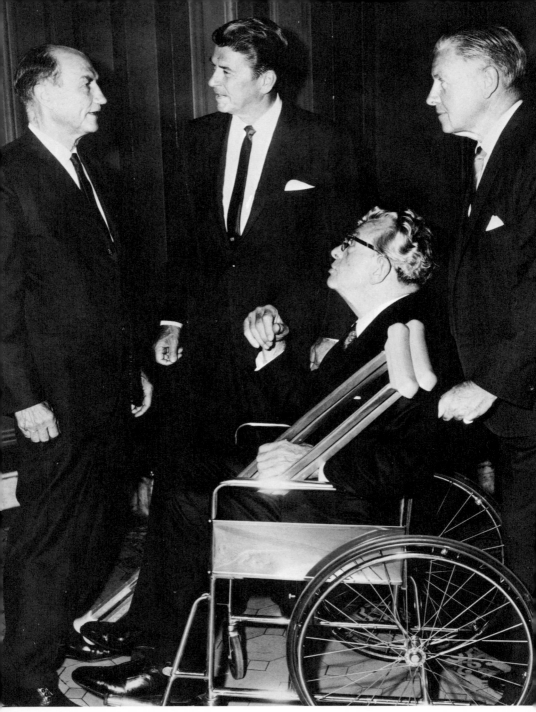

NEITHER A BROKEN HIP NOR A WHEELCHAIR CAN STAY THE MIGHTY DIRKSEN FROM HIS APPOINTED ROUNDS OF GETTING VOTES FOR HIS GOP PROGRAMS. SOME OF THE DEDICATED GOPERS ARE SENATOR STROM THURMOND, SOUTH CAROLINA; GOVERNOR OF CALIFORNIA, RONALD REGAN AND SENATOR GEORGE MURPHY, CALIFORNIA.

become as familiar to us and as accepted a part of our routine as the ever-present clock over the Presiding Officer.

"Senator Dirksen, is, indeed, a most vigorous and rugged man. But he is, as we all are, vulnerable to the inclemencies which beset the human species. That is something we would do well to remember after the shock of this accident has passed and when the ever-accommodating and willing Minority Leader returns to our midst.

"It is a source of great regret to all of us that Senator Dirksen must be subject to the discomfort and pain of the injury. It is reassuring to know, however, that Mrs. Dirksen will be nearby to comfort him . . . "

Senator Thomas H. Keuchel (R. Calif.) rose to add his condolences and said: "I simply rise to speak on the *Record* the hope that each of us has, that with the grace of the Supreme Being, a unique American leader and a great Republican leader will speedily mend, and then will return to carry on his great efforts in behalf of the American people."

Senator Bourke Hickenlooper (R. Iowa) rose and said: "We do expect to have him back soon. He is, indeed, a valiant warrior in the forefront of his party's battles, and in the forefront of the battles of American people for their rights and for the future of our country and its progress. We all wish him the best of luck and a speedy recovery. I think we can well anticipate, with a normal recovery, some rather pithy and descriptive remarks from him, when he comes back, about his experience in the hospital, and we probably will all be not only regaled but much better educated about hospital procedure when he returns to his labors and his duties. I do not mean to be facetious about that, but just practical, because as we all know, Everett has a descriptive capacity which leaves not much to doubt when it comes to matters of that sort."

He gets bouquets at any time he is awarded a special honor, interviewed, or makes a speech. Others rise to be sure what he has said is in the *Record*. Congressman Carl Albert (D. Okla.) is typical of those who point to Senator Dirksen with praise, as in his remarks in the March 3, 1966, *Record*: "The able and distinguished Minority Leader of the other body of this Legislature has been named the recipient of the Congressional Award of the Veterans of Foreign Wars of the United States for his outstanding work in Congress . . . Mr. Dirksen has served his nation and his state of Illinois with great distinction for thirty years. Prior to being elected to the Senate he sat in this body for many years and was an outstanding member of the House.

"I wish to point out that Senator Dirksen joins the most distinguished of Congressional company in receiving this Veterans of Foreign Wars Congressional Award. Last year the recipient was . . . the Honorable

The Golden Voice of The Senate

SURROUNDED BY A GROUP OF SENATE FRIENDS
AND RICHARD M. NIXON, DIRKSEN IS PROBABLY
EXPOUNDING ON THEIR LATEST STRATEGY. WITH
HIM ARE: SENATOR HUGH SCOTT, PENNSYLVANIA;
SENATOR BARRY M. GOLDWATER; SENATOR
GEORGE D. AIKEN, VERMONT AND SENATOR
THOMAS H. KEUCHEL, CALIFORNIA.

John McCormack. The first recipient was the distinguished Senator, Carl Hayden of Arizona, President Pro Tempore of the United States Senate."

Senator Winston L. Prouty (R. Vt.) compared Dirksen most favorably to Lincoln and Thomas Jefferson when he said on the floor of the Senate during discussions on the Civil Rights Bill: "One hundred and three years ago, when the House of this nation was divided, to serve the cause of freedom and to make our people one, a man came out of Illinois.

"One hundred and three years later, to open the doors of our national House and to serve the cause of freedom, another man has come out of Illinois.

"True it may be that no one man was responsible for the abolition of slavery. True it may be that no man is responsible for our statute to prohibit discrimination. But, without Lincoln there would have been no *Emancipation Proclamation,* and without Dirksen there would have been no Civil Rights Bill.

"From Jefferson to Johnson, from Lincoln to Dirksen, the roads are long and the journeys arduous."

Senator Mansfield also arose and praised the Illinois Senator: ". . . All senators have endured frustrations, disappointments, and inconveniences along the arduous trail which has led to this vote.

"But, I want to say in particular, of the distinguished Senator from Illinois, the Minority Leader (Mr. Dirksen), that this is his finest hour.

"His concern for the welfare of the nation, above personal and party concern, has been revealed many times in the Senate, but never before in so vital and difficult a context. The Senate and the whole country are in the debt of the Senator from Illinois."

Of course, he is not always praised: not when the opposition has felt the shock of his disapproval, particularly not if it involves a moral issue, and especially not if it further involves an office of trust. The brash pair of Kennedy Senators had their taste of the old maestro's condemnation in October, 1965 when they learned that neither their money, their publicity, nor their drive for power could awe Dirksen so that they could snap off a federal judgeship. It was Senator Edward Kennedy (D. Mass.) who tried very hard to get a federal judgeship for an old family friend and a long-time political worker for the Kennedy clan in the wards. When the name of Francis X. Morrisey was put up by Senator Ted Kennedy for the judgeship, it was revealed he was not properly qualified either educationally or in experience. Joseph Kennedy, Ted's father, it was reported in inner circles as well as in newspapers, had wanted this for his old buddy for a long time. But he could not even get his other son, John F. Kennedy, to do the chore when he was President. The appointment never came off and the request for this appointment had to be withdrawn.

A SENATOR'S
SENATOR

SENATOR DIRKSEN SEEMS TO BE GIVING SOME
SERIOUS INFORMATION TO CONGRESSMAN GERALD
R. FORD OF MICHIGAN WHO IS ALSO THE MINORITY
LEADER IN THE HOUSE; VICE PRESIDENT HUBERT
H. HUMPHREY AND SENATOR CARL HAYDEN OF
ARIZONA.

The Golden Voice of The Senate

Long before Dirksen arrived on the Senate scene, he was well known for his capacity for learning, absorbing and retaining a fantastic assortment of facts on a wide variety of issues and in great depth. His incisive mind was reflected in speeches which could calmly, quietly, but effectively slash at the foundations of governmental extravagances and inefficiencies. Such preparation for this role did not come about by sheer accident; Dirksen studied all of his life and is admired by his colleagues for his talent of digging for the facts on all bills. A long-time and close friend of his, Ben Regan, a leading financier and senior partner in Hornblower & Weeks-Hemphill, Noyes, New York, and Commissioner of The New York Port Authority, revealed many little known facts about the Senator. He said that when Dirksen first went to Congress he would work until about 8:00 p.m. on the Hill, then go to the Mayflower Hotel where he had a small room. There he would join Regan and sometimes another friend for a hamburger, coffee and an hour's conversation. Then up to his room he would go to beat on his old typewriter until about midnight, recording bits of poetry, rich prose or some snatch of rhetoric he particularly fancied during the day. Mr. Regan said he kept these in a notebook and today has filled sixty of them with these phrases.

The platform from which Everett Dirksen speaks as the Minority Leader is to him a sacred trust, as is

everything he tackles in Congress. He is as equally
dedicated to keeping that post from being tarnished
as he is the vaulted positions held by leaders of our
country, whether Democrats or Republicans, because
they are offices that spell the pride and dignity of
this land. And, as he has reasoned, the Democrats
hold several of them today, but the Republicans will
also gain their place in the sun. When they do, he does
not want them to have to spend the first year trying to
defend the very positions they fought so hard to be
elected to.

Most people see in Dirksen the symbol of fatherli-
ness, kindness, courtliness, wisdom and a highly depend-
able monument to law and order. Some have said that
Dirksen is one of the best known monuments in Washington not made of stone.

2

HE PRESIDENTS' SENATOR

■   Presidents from Franklin D. Roosevelt to Lyndon B. Johnson not only have felt the sting of the strength of Dirksen's leadership of the opposition force; they also have reasons to be deeply grateful to this articulate man when he considers Administration legislation worthy of his support. Presidents, Cabinet officers, colleagues and leaders from all walks of industrial and business life have come to him to get him to help establish a base for compromise.

Persuasion, wisdom and diplomacy are his tools; courage, fairness and integrity his creed.

He strongly opposed some of Roosevelt's "New Deal" but supported other parts; he supported much of his foreign policy because he felt the nation was in a time of peril and that the Presidency should not be impaired by a divided or bickering Congress. It was a grateful President Roosevelt whose National Recovery Act the popular Republican, then Congressman Dirksen, defended during the early years of F.D.R.'s tenure. His classic statement at that time, when he explained his position, will long be remembered: "The mind is no match with the heart in persuasiveness; constitutionality is no match for compassion."

The zenith of his statesmanship was reached in 1964 when he was responsible for cementing his colleagues in the action which moved the Civil Rights Bill through the Senate. He personally worked long hours with a variety of assistants, Cabinet officers and colleagues to clarify and ameliorate eighty amendments: these were vital keys to shaping the bill so it would be acceptable to the majority.

His comments about this bill were based on a quote from John Donne's seventeenth century *Devotions:* "Any man's death diminishes me, because I am involved in mankind." He parodied this by saying: "Whatever the color of a man's skin, we are all mankind. So every denial of freedom, of equal opportunity for a livelihood, or for an education, diminishes me. There is the moral basis for this legislation."

Commenting on his action, Negro columnist Carl T. Rowan said in his column in the *Washington Evening Star* of January 21, 1966: ". . . This is the man (Senator Dirksen) who in 1962 got almost no Negro support in his campaign for re-election . . . But two years later it was Everett Dirksen who wielded remarkable power among the thirty-three Senate Republicans and produced the key votes that enabled the Senate to invoke cloture and pass an historic civil rights law.

"It was a measure of Dirksen's bigness that he forgot and forgave what he thought was shabby treatment by Illinois' Negroes in 1962.

"The haggard, waspish, curly-haired Dirksen had explained in what he called a 'little sermon' why he had changed from a politician bitterly resentful of the 'Negro bloc' to a 'statesman' who had made possible one of the great moments in the nation's history.

SENATOR DIRKSEN GREETS HIS PARTY CHIEF,
PRESIDENT EISENHOWER AND INTRODUCES HIM
TO SENATOR ALEXANDER WILEY.

" 'No army can withstand the strength of an idea whose time has come,' he said. 'Civil rights—here is an idea whose time has come. Today the challenge is here. It is inescapable and the time has come to deal with it.' "

In the same column Rowan compared him to the late and much respected Senator, Arthur Vandenberg— as one of his colleagues had done on the floor. ". . . Yet, Vandenberg never wielded half of Dirksen's power nor gave to the nation half as much that is lasting and will be counted among the things that added up to its salvation. He's got a pretty big conscience that keeps fouling up his politics."

It is this conscience that tells Senator Dirksen that America is first and must be protected in all her power and glory to continue for hundreds of years in great dignity and respect.

He and his patience were sorely tried during the civil rights issue as, on June 10, 1964, on the Senate floor, he observed: "To those who have charged me with doing a disservice to my party because of my interest in the enactment of a good Civil Rights Bill— and there have been a good many who have made that charge—I can only say that our party found its faith in the Declaration of Independence in which a great Democrat, Jefferson by name, wrote the flaming words: 'We hold these truths to be self-evident: that all men are created equal.'

"That has been the living faith of our party. Do we forsake this article of faith now that equality's time has come or do we stand up for it and insure the survival of our party and its ultimate victory? There is no substitute for a basic and righteous idea. We have a firm duty to use the instruments at hand— namely, the cloture rule—to bring about the enactment of a good Civil Rights Bill."

When asked by a Chicago newspaper reporter why he was exerting himself to get the Civil Rights Bill through, particularly since he could not count on many votes from Illinois Negroes, the Senator said: "Sometime you have to do something for your country."

This action on his part is believed to have strengthened the hand of both moderates and liberals of his party.

He also reminded his Senate fellows that: "I am no Johnny-come-lately in this field (of civil rights). Thirty years ago, in the House of Representatives, I voted on the anti-poll tax and anti-lynching measures. Since then, I have sponsored or co-sponsored scores of bills dealing with civil rights."

His office is filled daily with all kinds of people, but particularly during the civil rights sessions he was literally plagued by clergy of all faiths, social workers, and militants. Mail poured in by the thousands indicating ten-to-one against the bill. He did not soften his stance one whit on how the bill should be worked out for the greatest good of the country—not even when some threatened violence if he did not "hurry" and get the bill passed. To this he remarked: ". . . A man is not fit to walk into this chamber as a United States Senator if he is to be bilked and influenced by that kind of argument to deter him from his duties under the laws and the Constitution."

Not only has Dirksen a monumental sense of fairness and responsibility, but he is keenly conscious of the role Congress must play with regards to the Presidency to assure its constructive place in history. His value lies in his wisdom to distinguish what is possible to obtain the best legislation that will stand the rigors of time and remain a permanent part of the constructive history of this country.

This conscience has always prompted him to defend Congress and the Presidency—at times fiercely—even to the point of risking unpopularity among his Congressional colleagues. Although he does not always agree with their thinking nor their decisions, he holds the Presidency, the Cabinet posts and the Supreme Court in great esteem and will not allow them to be defamed or bemeaned: to him they signify the highest offices of America. That they may be occupied by a Republican or Democrat is not the most significant point (though he certainly prefers the first): they are offices of this land and he seeks to maintain the respect due them. He risked the scorn of his Republican followers in

THE PRESIDENTS'
SENATOR

THE EISENHOWERS, THE NIXONS AND THE DIRK-
SENS GET TOGETHER IN AUGUST 1960 AS THE
REPUBLICAN ERA WAS NEARING ITS CLOSE.

the Senate by taking to the floor of the Senate in October, 1967 to rebuke Senator Thruston B. Morton (R. Ky.) and former National Chairman of the GOP. Senator Morton had strongly accused President Johnson of being "brainwashed by the military-industrial complex into seeking a military solution in Viet Nam . . ." Senator Dirksen declared in his rebuke: "You do not demean the President in the eyes of the people abroad because when you do you demean the prestige of this country. . . . It's a pretty small world with high-speed bombers, so let no one say our security is not involved."

It was Senator Dirksen who helped overcome Senate resistance to bailing out the United Nations by an emergency $100-million bond issue, and who helped make the Latin American Coffee Treaty during the Kennedy Administration. He sided with the President on these issues and many others which he felt were of value to the country's welfare in the international market.

During the Administration of Dwight D. Eisenhower, Dirksen, upon becoming Minority Leader of the Senate in 1959 (with the President's blessings), established easier liaison between the Congress and the President. At the Republican Convention in 1952, where Eisenhower was chosen to be the GOP standard-bearer, Dirksen had nominated Senator Robert Taft. In the interest of the party, however, he went to the General to assure him he would fight hard to help him

SENATOR DIRKSEN JOINS FELLOW SENATORS JOHN
SPARKMAN, FAR LEFT, AND MAJORITY LEADER
MIKE MANSFIELD, FAR RIGHT, AND THE THEN
VICE PRESIDENT, LYNDON B. JOHNSON, IN A MO-
MENT OF RELAXATION WITH VISITING WEST GER-
MAN CHANCELLOR, KONRAD ADENAUER. THIS
PICTURE WAS TAKEN APRIL 13, 1961.

win the election and to do a good job for this country. So well did they work together that he came to be considered the President's right arm.

But the golden-voiced orator of the Senate has also made Presidents wince with his incisive pronouncements against their policies and their bills. He lashed out at Kennedy's balance of trade deficit, the rising crime rate, his escalation of the Viet Nam war and his ". . . dangerous economic brinkmanship and the New Frontier's determination to make the 1960's the decade of debt, deficits and disasters . . ."

Dirksen denounced Johnson's welfare stance, his lack of leadership to win the Viet Nam war, his inability to show proper leadership in cleaning up crime in the streets and his do-nothing attitude about the reckless spending of the people's money.

Over the years, Presidents have experienced inconceivable joy when the powerful and effective Dirksen looked with favor upon their legislation; but, when Dirksen looked with disfavor, it has been excruciatingly painful.

As an editorial writer expressed it: ". . . Although highly sensitive to the necessity and values of intelligent scrutiny of the dominant party's activities, Dirksen, like many another enlightened lawmaker before him, places right above rank partisanship.

"Too many of our legislators, both state and national, put party first, Main Street second and the

GOVERNOR CLAUDE KIRK OF FLORIDA JOINS
SENATOR DIRKSEN IN FRONT OF ONE OF THE
SENATOR'S FAVORITE OIL PAINTINGS OF LINCOLN,
WHICH HANGS IN HIS OFFICE ON CAPITOL HILL.

general national good last . . .''

The basic philosophy that has permeated Senator Dirksen's career and ultimately elevated him to the enviable plateau of statesmanship was most aptly expressed in the March 1933 issue of *New Outlook,* a magazine in which the new Congressman Dirksen described what it was like to be a freshman Congressman in a three-to-one minority position: "What can a young, inexperienced, Republican Congressman, divested of all patronage, do for his country and his district in the midst of a three-to-one Democratic majority? . . . It is a stimulus to individual ego and conceit that might easily prompt a recital of good intentions and noble resolves. While this situation has its disadvantages, there is compensation in the fact that it permits much time for study and constructive attention to legislation. The function of the minority party, is after all, in the salutary influence which it can exercise in resolutely opposing things which are fundamentally wrong and supporting those measures which are right. Under such circumstances, opportunities for service are certain to arise . . .

"The belief is still extant that a loyal party man will oppose everything which the other party proposes, right or wrong. This is the doctrine of regularity carried to a vicious extreme. I do not believe that such a political gospel appeals to the citizenry of this country, particulary at a time when high taxes are eating out

THE PRESIDENTS'
SENATOR

PRESIDENT JOHNSON ADDRESSES THE SENATE
LEADERSHIP GROUP. HIS REMARKS SEEMED TO
HAVE GONE OVER WITH SENATOR MIKE MANSFIELD;
DIRKSEN APPEARS TO BE TAKING A DIMMER VIEW.

the nation's substance, when millions of unemployed are in a state of moral desperation, when banks continue to evaporate and business is in the doldrums. This is a time for the exemplification of citizenship and Americanism rather than partisanship, else how can we make any hopeful degree of progress out of this economic cataclysm?

"Our present problems are ethical and moral as well as economic. No one will contend that within this nation we cannot find men with sufficient vision and knowledge to fabricate feasible, practical and constitutional measures for the relief of business, agriculture, banking, transportation and other enterprises. The real problem lies in effecting a subordination of individual and group interest and in ironing out the real and fancied conflict of interests to the point where such measures can be inscribed on the statute books, and that problem is ethical rather than economic. The lush days of prosperity seem to have created within us a total incapacity for sacrifice, yet how can we reach firm ground without it?

"Now is a time for a new political credo. The New Deal requires moral and ethical as well as economic retrenchments and it will hold out a glorious promise only when those in political life will resolve that they can serve their constituencies best when they serve their country best."

Though this was written thirty-five years ago, such is the fiber of the Dirksen political philosophy. Many have added there are two other important facets of his political philosophy and they include his great gift at arbritration and his disdain for character assassination.

These are the qualities that Eisenhower saw and because of them he went out to Illinois in 1956 and campaigned for Dirksen's re-election, which he won by 400,000 votes. Twenty-four years previous Dirksen did not have a President campaigning for him, but he did have a very popular image in F.D.R. campaigning against him plus strong Democratic opposition. Not even the landslide victory of F.D.R. which inundated most Republicans in 1932 could swamp this almost lone survivor of the onslaught. Everett McKinley Dirksen won by 23,147 votes (1,000 more than F.D.R.) his first seat in the House—a seat to which he was returned as long as he wanted it. For sixteen years he served his constituents in the House until a serious eye ailment forced his temporary retirement (1949-51). But when he recuperated he ran for the Senate seat then held by the very popular Scott Lucas to whom all political prognosticators gave a wide margin of victory. The voters did not see it that way on the day of determination. Many have said it was a pity they had to choose between two such exemplary legislators; that they would be far better off to have both such statesmen in Congress. Both men from Illinois distinguished themselves and today Dirksen is remembered best perhaps for his ability to view impartially situations which threaten the freedoms or safety of Americans everywhere. He is cognizant of the value of keeping the image of America and its high offices on lofty pedestals but in a realistic stance. He strives to keep our leaders from being put in an embarrassing posture or being caught in awkward situations.

These are the ground rules the Senator seems to apply when working with the President and his staff. He not only keeps the minority party in a potent position, but such a working relationship allows his group far greater latitude and strength when it comes to defending or opposing legislation that affects the good of the people.

ONE OF THE MOST FAMED ACTS IN CONGRESS FOR
A FEW YEARS WAS WHEN CONGRESSMAN CHARLES
HALLECK (R., IND.) AND SENATOR DIRKSEN
TEAMED UP TO STAGE A RADIO SHOW SO THEY
ANSWER QUESTIONS FROM THE LISTENERS, PRE-
SENT THE LATEST ON LEGISLATIVE ACTIVITY AND
GENERALLY ALERT THE PUBLIC TO THE REPUBLI-
CAN POLICIES OF THE DAY. HERE THEY ARE FOL-
LOWING A LEADERSHIP MEETING AS THEY ANSWER
QUESTIONS FROM THE WASHINGTON PRESS CORPS.

THE GOLDEN VOICE OF THE U. S. SENATE

3

It is difficult to find anyone, whether Democrats, Republicans, Socialists, labor leaders, cab drivers, financial leaders, ambassadors and the like, especially around Washington, D.C., who has anything but admiration for Everett McKinley Dirksen, his leadership, his intelligence, his legislative ability, and, most of all, his outstanding sense of humor and his oratory. Whether they agree with him or not, they generally find little to criticize, because they get the distinct feeling he is the ultimate in patriotism.

Tourists who flock to the Hill are bitterly disappointed if they cannot see the Senator or hear him speak. They stand outside the Senate dining room to glimpse him; they pass his door in the Capitol, and some stand as long as possible just to see the Senator go by.

They rise from both sides of the aisles on both sides of the Hill to praise this man who for years has been an important factor in the milieu of the legislative arena. Though many disagree on some of his political and legislative stands, they respect him as a strong leader and an outstanding orator. Accolades are not just of recent origin; he has been receiving them for years and is one of the few politicians who really enjoys a warm relationship with a skeptical and highly critical press corps. Upon entering the race for his Senate seat in Illinois in 1950, he was heralded by many as one of the best campaigners and finest orators of the century.

The Golden Voice of The Senate

When he brings his large-framed body, like an over-sized rumpled gnome, up from his seat in the front row of the Republican side of the Senate to address the chamber, word spreads rapidly through the corridors. Most of his colleagues hasten to be in attendance and the galleries—both public and press—fill to the brim with eager spectators wanting to hear this remarkable speaker who, by all oratorical yardsticks, should not rate such a tremendous and spontaneous an audience.

His voice has a deep and rasping quality, but—coming from Everett Dirksen—this only enhances his charm. His manner of expression is that of a slow Southern-Midwestern drawl variety, but this provides the aura of courtliness. His remarks are always coated in eloquent language of a bygone era which, if attempted by any other, would evoke ridicule and criticism. But not for this Senator, who holds his audience so spellbound they dare not whisper for fear of missing some gem of humor or unique expressions about patriotism, motherhood, flowers, the flag, or numerous other subjects on which he discourses with utmost authority and wit. His tongue-in-cheek phrases are often self-abnegating or joshing, but never does he resort to anger, mud-slinging or tearing another down.

This part of his nature he explained in his 1933 article, when he commented about the problem of finding a platform on which to campaign in 1932. He

IN THE STUDIO WHERE DIRKSEN MADE HIS RE-
CORDINGS, HE GETS SOME INSTRUCTIONS FROM
RON COCHRAN AND ARCH LUSTBERG.

said: ". . . with unemployment increasing, with banks
popping throughout the country, business stagnant . . .
what could one say on behalf of Herbert Hoover and
against Franklin D. Roosevelt that would have any
appreciable effect?

"How could one successfully apologize for Republican leadership when the nation was bleeding from
wounds of the Depression? Moreover, what could one
say against the Democratic candidate for Governor of
Illinois, when in strict fact he was a clean, honorable
and upright citizen? Too many of the candidates on
both state and county tickets were close personal friends
and it seemed wholly unfair to say or do anything
to injure their candidacies that might be dictated by
political differences and considerations, rather than by
personal conviction. It was a difficult problem in
political strategy and quite often doubts arose as to
whether it was a sound and ethical course.

"I distinctly recall the occasion when, at an out-
door picnic of one of the Ward Clubs, I first enunciated
this political philosophy and assured the voters that our
problems were economic and appealed to citizenship
rather than partisanship. I had no stomach for hurling
real or fancied charges against the Democrats nor could
I convince myself that they were so bad and incompe-
tent as to require a thorough disinfecting before they
were prepared to sit in the seats of authority. This
seemed eminently acceptable to the Republicans who

THE GOLDEN VOICE OF
THE U. S. SENATE

ARCH LUSTBERG, EXECUTIVE WITH CHAPPELL MUSIC CO., NEW YORK, AND DIRECTOR OF THE RECORDING SESSIONS FOR THE SENATOR'S RECORDS, PRESENTS DIRKSEN WITH THE FIRST COPY OF "GALLANT MEN." WITH HIM IS JOHN CACAVAS, THE COMPOSER, CONDUCTOR AND ARRANGER OF THE BACKGROUND MUSIC FOR THE RECORDING.

59

The Golden Voice of The Senate

ntended to vote for Roosevelt and to the Democrats
who intended to vote for me."

But the Republicans felt Dirksen should have
heaped coals of fire upon all Democrats and so ad-
monished him; this did not stop him from sticking to
issues and using his magnificent voice and graciousness
so effectively that he won in spite of the admonishments.

Since that time he has enjoyed his colleagues'
appreciation of his ability to speak and appears to be
more impelled to entertain than most speakers, especially
legislators, which makes his presentation much more
palatable to the listener and much more persuasive.
Further, this is a speaker who is renown for having
done his homework and who is indeed a hard task-
master for himself, putting in a twelve-to-eighteen-hour
day.

One of the classics of all times concerning the
Senator's voice and his ability to sway his audience
came from Senator Mike Mansfield, the Senate Majority
Leader, and a close friend of Dirksen's. Mansfield rose
after many Senators had paid great tribute to Senator
Dirksen and almost eclipsed anything ever said by or
about Dirksen: "If only I possessed the eloquence of
the distinguished Senator from Illinois. If only I had
his wit and wisdom . . . his humor and his poetry . . .
scholarly erudition and homespun simplicity . . . Had
I these gifts, I would unlease them in orchestrated
expression of the great affection, respect, admiration

TONY SANDLER AND RALPH YOUNG ARE IMPOR-
TANT MEMBERS OF THE TEAM WHO INTERESTED
THE SENATOR IN RECORDING HIS VOICE. THIS IS
ONE OF THE THREE EARLY RECORDS HE MADE.

and esteem in which I hold the distinguished Minority Leader. I would weave with the words a magic spell over the Senate as he has done so many times. With words, I would lift the eyes of the Senators to the mountain peaks and the stars beyond, or I would lead them gently down a rustic road in Illinois. With words, I would lay bare the heart of a flower or pry open the fiery core of the atom that the Senate might appreciate the depth and breadth of the Senator from Illinois."

Congressman Albert W. Watson, who switched from the Democratic ranks in 1966 to run as a Republican from South Carolina, commented that Senator Dirksen could recite the alphabet and make it sound like the *Gettysburg Address,* while anybody else could recite the *Gettysburg Address* and it would sound like the alphabet by contrast. He contributes much of his success in winning his election in 1966, after serving two terms as a Democrat, to the fact that Senator Dirksen campaigned for him in South Carolina. He recalls that after the Senator spoke at one rally, crowds jammed around the platform to shake his hand; this included old, young, tiny tots, and all. A long-time Democrat friend of Watson's was in line and was extolling the magnificent speech the Senator had given. Having been mentioned a few times quite favorably in the Senator's speech, Congressman Watson was anxious to learn what she thought were the best parts. She replied: "I don't know because I don't remember a word he said, but his speech was simply grand, and I am for anything Senator Dirksen is for!"

He is known by a variety of affectionately be-
stowed names including "Honey Tonsils," "Buttered
Larynx," "The Grand Old King of the Senate," "The
Senate's Golden Voice," "The Capital's Foremost Fo-
rensic Mesmerizer," "The Old Growler," "The Rumpled Magician of the Metaphor," "Colorful Cornball,"
"Super Trouper of the Senate," "The Heartthrob of
the Medicare Crows," "Silver Throated Senator,"
"Organ Voice," "Sepulchral Baritone," "Pagliacci
of American Politics," and scores of others. But he
is not one to take offense at being called names.

When he received his "Grammy" award in May,
1968, on a television show, he said: "I have been the
target of a certain amount of levity concerning my
voice. I believe it was Mr. Hope (Bob) who said I
sounded like a duet between Tallulah Bankhead and
Wallace Beery. He also challenged the right of a
Senator to invade the sanctum sanctorum of show
business. Well, Mr. Hope, may I make my position
clear. I have been speaking for the record for thirty
years. I have merely moved from one Capitol to
another."

The Senator was referring to Capitol Records,
for which he made his award winning record, "The
Gallant Men," a collection of excerpts from famous
patriotic speeches and historical pronouncements. Arch
Lustberg, well known drama coach, and an executive
with Chappell & Co. Inc., Music Publishers, also a

The Golden Voice of The Senate

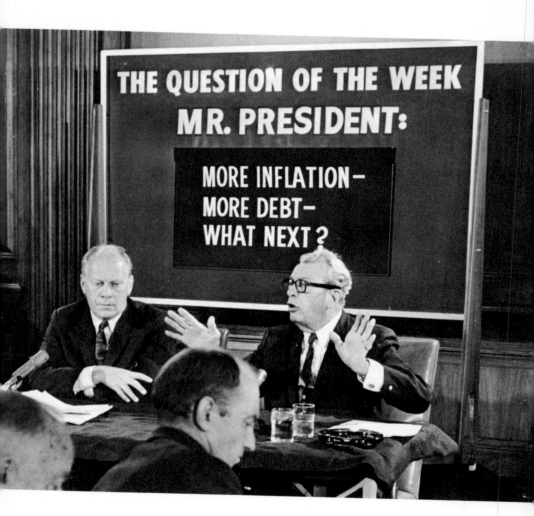

ANOTHER QUESTION OF THE WEEK GETS A STRONG
GOING OVER AS SENATOR DIRKSEN AND CON-
GRESSMAN GERALD R. FORD, MICHIGAN (HOUSE
MINORITY LEADER), FACE THE PRESS AT THEIR
REGULAR WEEKLY CONFERENCES.

friend of the Senator's, directed his recording sessions. He also directed the Senator when he made "Man Is Not Alone," and "At Christmas Time." Ron Cochran and Paul Jeffers, former ABC newsmen, wrote "Gallant Men" then joined forces with Arch. Arch commented: "Senator Dirksen and his recordings are grand happenings; a most refreshing projection into today's loud, harsh and often coarse entertainment world. When he speaks, one stops to listen."

"Gallant Men," released late in 1966, was an immediate hit, and made Everett Dirksen one of the top "best selling male vocalists" of the year, according to an industry survey. He ranked fifth ahead of Elvis Presley, Dean Martin and Bob Dylan. In winning the "Grammy" award, given annually by the National Academy of Arts and Sciences for the best documentary recording, he was in distinguished company with other "Grammy" winners: Yehudi Menuhin, Ravi Shankar, Lou Rawls, Cannonball Adderly, Bobbie Gentry and Glen Campbell.

The Senator had been approached by another company earlier to make some recordings, but, he noted, he was ". . . willing to sign, except they wanted me to also read *Winnie the Pooh* and *Peter Rabbit.* I do not think it would be consonant with my work in public service to be known as a reader of nursery rhymes."

It was an old friend, Arnold C. Pedersen of Minneapolis, who in 1963 sent a postcard urging the enator to ". . . record that rich, resonant voice of ours for posterity while you are still here to do it . . ." This prompted Dirksen to consider the possibility, and hree years later he made his first recording on a professional level.

The recordings made the Senator even more popular with the masses. In January, 1968, when he was Grand Marshall of the Tournament of Roses, he was observed by a 20th Century-Fox studio boss who listened to him speak and watched how he handled people. Finally the Fox executive burst out admiringly: 'What a ham! What a winning way that guy has with people! We should sign him. We could turn him into another Will Rogers!''

The movie executive had seen nothing if he had not witnessed Dirksen's television performance with Red Skelton—from whom he stole the show—and his video tour of the Capitol, his favorite historic building. Those were understated masterpieces of showmanship.

Life magazine, in its March 26, 1965, issue, declared that Senator Dirksen: ". . . must be numbered among those very few Senators who have influenced his colleagues with public utterances. Because he has been impelled to lead, not simply enforce, party discipline—to ask, at times, for attitudes and concepts of duty more adventurous and controversial than many of his colleagues would have adopted on their own—he has been impressive indeed on those rare occasions when he has risen in serious appeal on the floor.

THE GOLDEN VOICE OF
THE U. S. SENATE

THE SENATOR ENJOYS MEETING HIS ILLINOIS
CONSTITUENTS, AND ESPECIALLY LIKES TO AUTO-
GRAPH HIS RECORDS. HERE THREE VOTERS FROM
ILLINOIS AND A GUEST FROM MICHIGAN BASK IN
THE CHARM OF THE MASTER: TOM McDONALD,
DANVILLE, ILLINOIS; PAUL FRIEDLAND, CHICAGO;
WALTER M. FISCHER, CHICAGO AND LEROY WHITE,
DETROIT.

"Dirksen's wonderfully ornate speaking style has tended to obscure his less dramatic political talents. His splendiferous employment of words, his pauses, his loving refusal to relinquish vowels, his shameless partition of syllables, his unctuous use of the lower registers are all effects which could have sprung direct from the declamatory nineteenth century theatre of Edwin Booth, James O'Neill and Maurice Barrymore. But he is a legislative technician of a high order, a practiced and sagacious political thinker and must now be considered— if only for his classic marshalling of votes for the Civil Rights Act—one of the few real leaders of either party the Senate has known in the last half century."

In 1966, *Look* magazine, in its July 26th issue, heaped more praise upon the distinguished Senator, who was described: ". . . as a leader of the very minority Everett McKinley Dirksen ought to be politically impotent. Instead he's the Senate's uncrowned potentate. When he rises to speak, Senators gather for aisles around to hear. And once begun no one can foretell where (or when, or if) that speech will end. And ah, the sound of it . . . the thunderous sonority, the husky whisper . . . now he astonishes his colleagues with a pirouette . . . hushes them with a pause . . . then whoosh! fact after point-scoring fact, yet never a glance at a note."

When asked about not using notes, Senator Dirksen replied: "I always extemporize. I love the diversions,

THE GOLDEN VOICE OF
THE U. S. SENATE

AT THEIR WEEKLY PRESS CONFERENCES SENATOR
DIRKSEN AND HIS COUNTERPART IN THE HOUSE
OF REPRESENTATIVES GERALD R. FORD, MICHI-
GAN ARE OPEN FOR QUESTIONS OF ALL TYPES.

the detours. Without notes you may digress . . . you may dart . . . and after you've taken on an interrupter, you don't have have to flounder around with a piece of paper trying to find out where in the Hell you were.''

Another graphic description of the Senator's speaking ability came from *Time* magazine, September 14, 1962: "Whence comes this counterpoint that shivers the crystals into a new shimmering song? It comes from the man behind the desk—a big-handed, big-boned man with a lined, cornfield face and greying locks that spiral above him like a halo run amok. He speaks, and the words emerge in a soft, sepulchral baritone. They undulate in measured phrases, expire in breathless wisps. He fills his lungs and blows word-rings like smoke. The sentences curl upward. They chase each other around the room in dreamy images of Steamboat Gothic. Now he conjures moods of mirth—now of sorrow. He rolls his bright blue eyes heavenward. In funereal tones, he paraphrases the Bible ('Lord, they would stone me . . .') and church bells peal. 'Motherhood,' he whispers, and grown men weep. 'The Flag!' he bugles, and everybody salutes. No one who has ever seen and heard this performance will ever forget it.

This oratory is not just something that gets attention at campaign rallies or on the Senate floor. At the occasional meetings of Congressional leaders and the President behind closed doors the room falls silent when Dirksen rises to speak. One of the privileged few who

70

can observe these proceedings among extroverted legislators and politicians is Robert Parker, the popular
maitre de of the Senate dining room. He arranges the
private get-togethers and remains to attend the needs
of the lawmakers in a serious session.

"I have seen a lot of politicians come and go, but
I have yet to see one who, when he rises to speak,
automatically commands such attention as Senator
Dirksen," Parker commented. "Why, they don't even
whisper occasionally as they do sometimes when others
speak. He is truly a commanding presence and a great
man. He makes a tremendous impression with his
mannerisms, his voice and his wit. Anyone he meets is
immediately captivated by his gentleness, his considerate-
ness and his warmth. He never raises his voice in anger,
nor do you hear him speak evil of his fellow man. I
have watched him and note that while his countenance
is a pleasant, kind one, he does not laugh a lot or
smile, but seems more to have the world problems on
his mind, and I think people sense this and the world
smiles for him."

4

RROUNDED BY YOUNG MEN AND WOMEN AT A
CEPTION FOR THE GOP INTERNS, DIRKSEN
TURES TO THEM ON THE MORES OF LEGISLA-
E PURSUIT, ON PATRIOTISM AND THE EXCITE-
NT OF BEING A MEMBER OF THE NOBLE BODY
CONGRESS. THE LADIES, YOUNG, MIDDLE-AGED
O OLD ALL LIKE TO HEAR THIS MAN TALK.

CHAMPION OF THE PEOPLE

■ A constant guardian of the people's individual rights and wants, Senator Dirksen is a rare breed of political man. He always thinks in terms of people in relation to the dignity, the might and the continuing success of this country. If there appears to be a conflict between a majority of the people and the aims and needs of the country as a whole, Dirksen is most likely to stand by his country and do his best to protect it, and for this he has often stood the outrage of colleagues and voters.

Ben Regan explains, in describing Dirksen, that "He has a kind of patriotism that transcends all other considerations. In fact, perhaps if his patriotism had not gotten in the way Ev would be far better off now than what he is. He has a little country house near Herndon, Virginia, that is mortgaged and a little beach house in Florida—also mortgaged.

"It is surprising to many when they learn that Ev never owned a home until in the past few years. He has fought vigorously for law and order; helped shape the major Civil Rights Bill; wrote the Test Ban Treaty; and since Roosevelt days has played a major role in aiding every President to a large measure on his foreign policy proposals. He has the utmost confidence in the office of the Presidency, especially because it was the people who put him there as their leader."

The Senator has always decried the philosophy of deficit spending and sending too much money abroad.

SENATOR DIRKSEN ENJOYS BEING THE POINT OF A GOOD JOKE. HERE HE IS FOLLOWING A SAINTS AND SINNERS' LUNCHEON AT WHICH HE WAS THE ''FALL GUY.'' HE AUTOGRAPHS A PICTURE OF HIMSELF.

He says: ". . . let us have moderation, prudence and reason in the conduct of our national and local governmental affairs." His frequent and colorful reminders to the opposition party about their fiscal and financial difficulties are good for several national stories for weeks afterwards. He emphasizes his anti-tariff-cutting views and calls upon the law makers not to weaken the financial and trade resources of the United States to a degree that any nation or group of nations can dominate U. S. policy. The lawmakers, he feels, should be farsighted enough to strengthen the American system by adopting laws calculated to foster America's strength and economic growth, rather than submissively accept policies which chiefly contribute to strengthening other nations at our expense.

He hauled the Democrats over the coals in one of his articles, "Seduction by Statistics," which was put in the *Congressional Record* and in which he classified Sargent Shriver as a distinguished practitioner of the statistical avalanche: "The avalanche device is triggered when Mr. Shriver is questioned at press conferences about instances of what he defends as high-spirited mayhem or arson in his scandal-ridden, politically manipulated Job Corps, which is part of the federal poverty program.

"On one occasion last fall, he called down a tumbling mass of statistics which rolled end over end, at express-train speed, to engulf the reporters. It included data ranging from the annual cost of keeping an

THE MASTER OF VERBAL EXCHANGE PONDERS A JEST TOSSED AT HIM BY
SENATOR HOWARD H. BAKER, JR., HIS SON-IN-LAW.

CHAMPION OF
THE PEOPLE

THE MORE THE SENATOR CAN DO TO MAKE THE
YOUNG GENERATION CONSCIOUS OF THEIR HERIT-
AGE THE BETTER. HERE HE PRESENTS A FLAG TO
A GROUP OF HIGH SCHOOL STUDENTS FROM HIS
HOME STATE.

inmate in the Illinois penitentiary at Menard to the median consumption of fish, classified as to weight and species, by seals in the Seattle Zoo.

"When the last rush subsided, the shaken questioner was sorry he had asked the little question that started it all, namely: 'How much more does it cost to keep a boy in the Job Corps than in Harvard University?'

"The question," Dirksen continued, "was buried in the statistical snow-job. There it will remain forever unless a shift in the political glacier opens a crevasse and exposes it to view."

Always one to highlight the amusing side while applying the needle, Senator Dirksen went on to remind his readers while discoursing on his favorite subject —government waste—that "A phantom statistic which even compels its compilers to smile is that showing 'the rising productivity of government employees.' There are, of course, many conscientious, hard-working government employees among the myriads, but they are all supported by the work of someone else. What could they produce but statistics?

"An old favorite is what might be called the Cheshire Statistic. It is pulled out of the air like a magician producing a bowl of goldfish. Such a statistic was the basis for the charge during the 1960 Presidential campaign that 'seventeen million Americans go to bed hungry every night.'" Not four million, or 18.1 million, but seventeen million exactly, the Senator chided.

CHAMPION OF
THE PEOPLE

SENATOR DIRKSEN ENTERTAINS RED SKELTON AT
A LUNCHEON ON CAPITOL HILL ARRANGED BY HIS
FAVORITE PARTY GIVER, ROBERT PARKER, THE
MAITRE DE OF THE SENATE DINING ROOM.

"Unless many of them were reducing, that seemed to indicate a deplorable breakdown in a public relief system which was even then the most gigantic ever conceived. But then, President Johnson raised the figure two years ago to thirty-five million. It hung on the campaign air a while like its predecessor and then faded gently from view."

In his crusade to champion the people's cause, Senator Dirksen finds constant refreshment of ideas, and views in his continuous association with the people. His is a gregarious personality, a faculty which is tremendously valuable in helping him maintain contact with the people for whom he is working. He has often said that "One of the real pleasing and one of the most joyful things that can happen to you is when bellboys, waiters and waitresses come up and shake hands with you because they have been following what is going on. These are the people who, singularly, cannot help themselves but who are out there working hard to make a living with their eye on better things as they advance educationally by their own strivings."

Everett Dirksen knows quite a lot about hard work. His reputation for being one of the hardest working and most informed parliamentarians of his time has its roots in the poor industrious immigrant element of Illinois. He milked the half-dozen cows, tended the other livestock, hoed weeds, and carried pails of milk to customers on notched broomsticks from the small two-acre farm, with which his mother, besides taking in sewing and washing, sustained the family. He worked in a variety of jobs to help put himself through three years of college at the University of Minnesota. He has never lost his touch with the people nor his sense of the rugged quality of a life of hard work and doing for one's self.

Dirksen has apparently enormous rapport with the Germans, the Polish, the Jews, the Swedes and other ethnic groups; but, it is the Irish that he pleases especially when each year he can be counted upon to suggest the introduction of a bill in Congress to unite the whole of Ireland. They love that, and for a while the British Ambassador squirms because if the bill ever got to the floor of Congress it might just be passed.

When people come to his office he listens to them. They come for everything from an autograph and a shy glimpse of their favorite Senator to doing a little desk pounding. One group decided to expound its dissatisfaction with the high cost of federal spending. The Senator listened calmly and thanked them for coming. He then sat down and wrote Armond L. Lyman, Executive Director of the Illinois State Chamber of Commerce:

"Your representatives called on me and made very strong statements about federal spending and what I should do about it. . . . Now, I know there are eighty-five projects in the State of Illinois being supported by federal funds. I feel it would be most helpful if you

SENATOR DIRKSEN AND CONGRESSMAN GERALD
R. FORD, MINORITY LEADER OF THE HOUSE, PARRY
QUESTIONS FROM NEWSPAPER REPORTERS AND
TV MEN ABOUT PUBLIC SAFETY—A QUESTION OF
CONSIDERABLE IMPORTANCE TO THESE TWO
LEADERS.

THE JOHNSON-HUMPHREY ADMINISTRATION GETS
A GOING OVER FROM THE REPUBLICAN LEADER-
SHIP AS SENATOR DIRKSEN AND GERALD R. FORD
MEET THE PRESS ON THE QUESTION OF THE HIGH
PRICE OF THE DEMOCRATIC ADMINISTRATION.

would circularize your representatives and let them decide which ones they would like to have eliminated in order to carry out their express desire to cut federal spending."

Ben Regan said that Dirksen had no more major problems on the subject because Illinois constituents were, no doubt, thinking about cutting the federal spending in states other than Illinois.

In one of his more recent patriotic speeches on the floor he upheld the sovereignty of the individual states: "The Constitution guarantees every state a republican form of government. We have a republican form of government in this country, because it is representative. . . . That is the issue. It will not die. I do not propose to let it die.

"I love this country. My parents came from the old country. I went to school in overalls. I lost my father at the age of five. Drew Pearson was right this morning when he referred to me as the driver of a bakery truck. Yes, I was.

"Show me the country that will give any humble person the opportunity that this country does. I do not want it eroded; I do not want it soiled; I do not want it impaired. I want no court to destroy this great inheritance that has come from men who signed the *Declaration of Independence,* who vouchsafed to us the greatest government on the face of the earth, and for which, and because we hope to maintain its perpetuity, we have boys twelve thousand miles from home.

EVERYONE WHO COMES TO WASHINGTON WANTS
TO VISIT THE MINORITY LEADER, AND THE ASTRO-
NAUTS ARE NO DIFFERENT. HERE THEY EXPLAIN
THEIR SPACE SHIP AND PROGRAMS.

"I say to Senators—mark it well—'You have not heard the last of this.' It will be tragic indeed when we have to campaign and say 'We are sorry; we tried to make you understand, but we could not' and so we can only say 'you do not love the people. You do not trust them.'

"May it never be said of me that I quailed in the endeavor to keep my trust in the people and keep intact the power which the people reserved to themselves in 1787, until they are prepared to forfeit it to the central government in Washington."

In his way he tries desperately to keep his sacred covenant with the people. Thus, it is with deep sincerity when he says: "I could not think of anything pleasanter than to have some humble citizen meet me in the street and say to me, 'You made some telling marks in the cause of civil liberty in your time and generation.' That would be enough for me."

CHAMPION OF
THE PEOPLE

THE SENATOR GENERALLY WINDS UP THE LONG
SESSION OF CONGRESS BY GATHERING HIS FAMILY
AND OFFICE STAFF AROUND FOR A DINNER IN HIS
CAPITOL OFFICE. HIS DAUGHTER JOY BAKER, IS
CENTER FRONT AND HIS WIFE SITS TO HIS RIGHT.
ROBERT PARKER, MAITRE DE OF THE SENATE DIN-
ING ROOM GENERALLY ARRANGES THE AFFAIRS.

E THE SENATOR CAPTURES THE AFFECTION
STAUNCH DEMOCRAT, MRS. WARREN MAG-
ON, WIFE OF THE SENATOR FROM WASHINGTON.

5

DIRKSEN AND THE DAMSELS

■ There is no doubt as to who are the favorite damsels in the life of Senator Dirksen. Also, there is no doubt that a large majority of females everywhere are completely fascinated by the Senator and—regardless of party—have an abiding affection for this man. His image evokes a wide range of feminine responses, from unabashed girl-man pursuit to adoring adolescents, who, upon his debut as a recording star, discovered him as their new type of male hero worship. They loudly proclaimed their allegiance to this new performer by wearing Dirksen buttons, swooning over his records and chasing him to get his autograph. The buttons they wore declared: "Ev, we luv you," "Ev, you melt me," "You leave me limp, Ev," and other similar phrases generally reserved for the adulation of some young singing star.

He is pursued for autographs at airports, in the halls of Congress, on the streets and at parties. One charming fifteen-year-old girl accosted the Senator in the Capitol and told him she thought he was great and asked: "Why can't you be President?" The Senator smiled and said: "The people in their wisdom choose our leaders according to our Constitutional procedure."

Youngsters are always bringing him things. One child brought him her favorite Troll doll because its grey, fluffy, flowing tresses reminded her of the Senator's own celebrated curly "mop." He accepted the gift graciously and still has it sitting on the mantel in his

SENATOR MARGARET CHASE SMITH PRESENTS
DIRKSEN WITH A PICTURE OF THE LATE SENATOR
ROBERT TAFT, WHOM SENATOR DIRKSEN NOMI-
NATED FOR THE PRESIDENCY IN 1952.

DIRKSEN AND
THE DAMSELS

DIRKSEN GREETS OLD FRIENDS, SENATOR AND
MRS. MIKE MANSFIELD. BOTH THE MANSFIELDS
ARE ADMIRERS OF THE SENATOR. HIS OTHER LADY
FRIENDS ARE: MRS. DIRKSEN, FAR LEFT; HIS
DAUGHTER JOY, AND FAR RIGHT, SENATOR MAR-
GARET CHASE SMITH.

Minority Leader's office. Once a timid young tourist left him a sandwich outside his door with a note scrawled in a child's handwriting that said: "I know you are busy and I thought maybe you could share my lunch since you probably can't get out to eat. Please come to see us. We live in Baltimore. Happy mayonnaise."

His office is deluged with letters from women wanting locks of his hair, asking favors of all sorts, sending him flowers or flower seeds or asking for seeds. Some have even asked him to make records for them. They swarm around him at parties and are not bashful about asking him for a kiss. One woman approached him at a reception and she told him she was a baby when he first campaigned and he did not kiss her then. "So," she said, "how about making up for it now?" He happily obliged. He has often said that ladies are delighted to receive a kiss, and he felt it was a delight to kiss any charming lady. "And," he adds, "they're all charming."

They ask his advice on a variety of subjects, but many are interested in his gardening capabilities and want to know what he does about a number of problems related to horticulture. They are anxious either to get some of his marigold seeds or to send him some of theirs to plant. His keen interest in the marigold is widely known because for years he has extolled its beauty and virtues on the floor of the Senate to interest his colleagues in naming the marigold our national flower. Each time he takes to the podium on the subject, he is swamped with letters from flower lovers everywhere.

When these women are unable to see, approach or have an audience with the Senator, they appeal to their own state Senators or Congressmen, or stand outside Dirksen's offices in the Capitol or the Old Senate Office Building to glimpse him as he goes by. If he passes a group of people he always stops briefly to say "hello" or to make some typically delightful Dirksen remark.

A woman once said to him, "Senator, guess where you first saw me?"

Dirksen replied: "Maybe it was in the Garden of Eden."

There is no deprecating, smart manner, but heavy eyebrows raised in feigned surprise, and clear blue eyes fixing one with a cherished look—unmistakably shows he is gently joshing in good clean fun.

When they cannot personally contact Senator Dirksen, some women have appealed to his handsome, vigorous young son-in-law, who was elected to the Senate in 1966 from Tennessee, and who enjoys an excellent relationship with his famed father-in-law. Some of his constituents report their disappointment in not getting to see Dirksen to Howard Baker: Each wishes him to soothe their feelings by sending her a

WITH HIS FAVORITE LEADING LADY, LOUELLA
CARVER DIRKSEN.

DIRKSEN AND
THE DAMSELS

SEN. DIRKSEN MAKES IT A REAL FAMILY AFFAIR
AT A BIRTHDAY PARTY FOR HIM: LEFT TO RIGHT:
LONG-TIME FRIEND BEN REGAN;CONGRESSMAN
BILL WAMPLER (R. VA.) , MRS. BEVERLY BAKER
PATESTIDES; SENATOR HOWARD J. BAKER (R.
TENN.), SON-IN-LAW OF THE SENATOR'S; MRS.
BAKER, THE SENATOR'S DAUGHTER; MRS. DIRK-
SEN, THE SENATOR; MRS. MARY BAKER WAMPLER
AND MICHAEL PATESTIDES, MRS. WAMPLER AND
MRS. PATESTIDES ARE SISTERS OF SEN. DIRKSEN'S
SON-IN-LAW, SEN. BAKER.

lock of Dirksen's hair. His hair—a shock of grey curls that most often has the unruly appearance of a frothy halo—has created almost as much comment as his distinctive voice. Were Senator Baker to attempt to fill all requests for a lock of his father-in-law's hair, the latter would be scalped in a week!

How does the most important lady in Dirksen's life take all of this adulation for her spouse? Louella Carver Dirksen, a girl from his home town of Pekin, Illinois, takes all of it in her jolly stride. She is the one who helped this big bear of a man, to whom she is greatly devoted, along the road from his bakery in Pekin to one of the highest positions a man can achieve. She has been right in the thick of things from the very beginning, encouraging him in everything he wanted to accomplish.

Everett Dirksen first saw Louella Carver when he was looking for a princess to play to his princely role in *A Thousand Years Ago,* a play he wrote with his friend, Hubert Rupp, for Pekin's 1923 centennial celebration. He had written two other plays with Hubert, one, *Chinese Love,* which they sold for $300 and split the munificent sum—the only literary endeavor for which Dirksen realized any financial gain at that time. The other play was *A Slave With Two Faces.* Dirksen had already written about one hundred short stories and five novels by that time—without success.

They had a hard time finding just the right girl

DIRKSEN AND
THE DAMSELS

TEENAGERS FLOCK AROUND AT HIS MARIGOLD
PLANTING SESSION.

for their princess until one day, Dirksen was with a group sipping sodas in a drug store. One of the boys pointed to a very pretty girl walking across the street: "Hey! There goes your princess!" Dirksen looked, jumped up and ran over to ask her to play the part. She said she would have to ask her mother. So did circumstances bring Everett Dirksen a lifelong leading lady: they were married in 1927.

His princess presented him with his only child, Denise Joy, in 1929; he then had two battling on his side. Both drove him around the State of Illinois on campaign tours so he could either read, sleep, or generally refresh himself for his next speaking engagement. When Joy was old enough, she passed out campaign literature, took notes for him and, when she gained skills, substituted for his secretary.

It is said that his favorite ladies drove him about 250,000 miles in his 1950 campaign for the Senate, during which time he made 1,500 speeches.

In his home state he is constantly pressed for time to fulfill all speaking engagements; he hates to turn anyone down. He loves church suppers, the county fairs and other informal gatherings in his state. Unlike most politicians at church suppers, instead of just shaking hands, he gets in the kitchen and helps the "girls" wash the dishes. They call him the talkin'est man in Tazewell County.

Occasionally, when asked about his talking, Mrs. Dirksen smiles and says affectionately, "Oh, Ev just loves to talk, but I don't pay any attention because I've heard it all before." If her husband is within ear-shot of such a remark, he feigns sadness: "Now, Toots, you know that's not true." Of course, it is hard for any woman to understand how one can live with a man for forty-one years and not have heard everything he knows many times over—especially his jokes. But Louella Dirksen realizes she has a most unusual man in her household.

Mr. Dirksen says of his wife: "She is a most for-bearing lady." He frequently refers to her as "the boss." She is constantly alert to his every need and tries to watch his health most carefully.

Their day begins usually about 5:00 a.m., they discuss his ideas, and often he dictates memos to her. After a turn around his flower garden, which includes checking the many birdhouses he builds for a hobby, he breakfasts and is off to his office in the Capitol. He arrives at about 9:00 a.m. to put in a twelve- to eighteen-hour day.

Mrs. Dirksen is considered one of his best cam-paigners, and he speaks glowingly of her at all times, but he does like to comment in his speeches that "I seldom get my way either at home or in the Senate." He added once: "But, life is meant to make adjust-ments in order to get as near a consensus in the party as is possible."

He tells an amusing story about Mrs. Dirksen calling him down when one evening at home he picked

The Golden Voice of The Senate

SENATOR AND MRS. DIRKSEN ARE JOINED BY MR. AND MRS. BEN REGAN, AND FAR RIGHT, MR. WARD QUAAL, PRESIDENT OF WGNTV. MR. REGAN, PARTNER OF HORNBLOWER & WEEKS — HEMPHILL-NOYES, AND HIS WIFE HAVE FOR YEARS GIVEN A SURPRISE BIRTHDAY PARTY FOR SENATOR DIRKSEN WHOSE BIRTHDAY IS JANUARY FOURTH.

MRS. FRANCES APPEL, A DEVOTED SECRETARY IN
THE SENATOR'S OFFICE, GETS THE JOB OF CLEAR-
ING THE MAIL URGING FOR PRAYERS IN SCHOOLS.

up the telephone and said: "Yes, Jack, No, Jack I don't think so . . ." When he hung up his wife asked to whom he was speaking. "Jack Kennedy," Senator Dirksen replied.

"Why, Ev! That's the President of the United States! You should certainly not address him in any such informal manner!"

As the Senator later commented: "Mrs. Dirksen scolded me soundly for using such a familiar form of address. So, two weeks later when I was at a meeting at the White House I brought up this subject and told the President about my scolding. I said: 'Mr. President, my wife thought I committed a breach of etiquette when I called you by your first name the other night.'

"The President said: 'Why Ev, who more than you has the right?'"

This made the Senator feel better, as he not only had known Kennedy since his arrival in the House, but had helped instruct him in 1960 on how to project his voice and be more effective in speaking—even though Dirksen was a Nixon campaigner. Kennedy, a fellow Senator, needed help with his elocution and had solicited the aid of Dirksen; the elder statesman could not see how he could possibly refuse him.

On the subject of women, Dirksen's mother plays a dominant role. He holds that his religious, political and moral philosophy had a good foundation laid by his mother's teachings and in her disciplining of her family. "There are some things" he states, "you get with your mother's milk, and among them is the recognition of moral principles. . . . I come of immigrant stock. My mother stood on Ellis Island as a child of seventeen, with a tag around her neck directing that she be sent to Pekin, Illinois. My saintly mother helped build a church and then took her brood there. We had to walk two miles, and that is a long way for a youngster of three or four to toddle. You knew nothing about automobiles or conveyances, but there you learned prayer, and you learned it at your mother's knee and you learned it in school."

His mother, who married a German immigrant, Johann Frederick Dirksen, helped build the wooden frame Second Reformed (Calvinist) Church in Pekin. Her children were all born in that little town and went to that church. Her first son was named Benjamin Harrison Dirksen—a proper name for the son of a staunch Republican, as was Mr. Dirksen. He named his second sons—twins—Everett McKinley and Thomas Reed (then Speaker of the House). His father died when they were five, and Mrs. Dirksen intensified her small truck farming on their two-acre plot to help feed and clothe her family.

It was his mother who encouraged her boys to work hard and study. Everett seemed to be the one more interested in books and in listening to debaters of the day; the others were more anxious to go to work and bring in money for the family as soon as they could. However, Everett went to work very soon and brought in $55 a month, all of which he turned over to his mother. But he kept on studying and hoping. He worked his way through three years of the University of Minnesota doing all sorts of jobs, from selling patent medicines to farmers to taking ads for the *Minneapolis Tribune.* His was an eighteen-hour day most of the time. Then World War I intervened and he went to the front, first as a cavalryman (because he had a kind face, he often jests), then as an observer with the balloonists (because he had good balance, he says). He returned home to try several business ventures, all of which were sad failures except the bakery business which his brothers had started. He received his law degree by studying nights at the Washington School of Law after he came to Washington as a Congressman.

Of the women in his life, there is one young lady who can innocently cut her "Gramps" down to her size, particularly since she has no true realization of his importance. Cynthia Baker, now twelve, daughter of Dirksen's daughter Joy and Senator Howard Baker, has no qualms about telling her Gramps he talks a little too much to please her at times. One night at the dinner table he was discussing some subject at great length, when Cynthia, watching her grandfather's performance, piped up: "Gramps, you sound just like Mr. Ed. (the TV personality)." That stopped the

IRENE ALLEN, THE MISS HOT DOG OF 1960 PRE-
SENTS THE SENATOR WITH HER OWN SPECIAL
BRAND OF "HOT DAWG."

great statesman in his verbal tracks. Once when asked
by a reporter what she thought of her father and
grandfather both being in the Senate, she replied:
"I think they travel too much."

Cynthia and her brother Darek Dirksen Baker,
now fifteen, came to Washington when their father
was elected to the Senate. Cynthia, along with the
other children, was asked on her first day in civics
class to name three people in Congress, if they could.
When it came her time, she stood up and said:
"Daddy, Gramps and Uncle Bill." This stopped the
proceedings, as few children had even one relative in
Congress, much less three. "Uncle Bill" is Congressman William Wampler (R. Va.), who married her
aunt, Mary Elizabeth Baker.

All the ladies in Senator Dirksen's offices are fans
of his. His right arm is Mrs. Glee Gomien, who
handles the front office for the Senator with tremendous
aplomb and grace which, in view of the vast number of
people who want to see the Senator, would stagger any
diplomat. She once told a reporter, when asked what
was the first thing she did when she started her week,
"On Mondays I smile, because by the end of the week
I may have forgotten how." She, like her boss, never
seems to get ruffled or out of sorts with the throng that
files through or the questions she has to answer.

One of the most amusing incidents about Dirksen
and the damsels—and perhaps his most embarrassing—

was one which made national headlines and gave his press friends a field day. The noted Claire Booth Luce was before the Senate to be confirmed so she could serve the United States as Ambassador to Brazil. Her appointment had caused some furor in several areas and there was haranguing for many days about it. Weary of the flurry of opposition and the embarrassment to the lady involved, Senator Dirksen one day finally rose to his feet in an appeal to put an end to this bickering and go ahead and appoint the lady. Toward the end of his comments he said: "Why thresh an old bale of hay or beat an old bag of bones?" He did not mean any disrespect, but did not consider how this might sound to his rivals at the moment. The Senate nearly fell apart—much of it with laughter.

Everett Dirksen is always the highlight of any event. The press clubs particularly like to have him as their guest, and no Republican conclave would be complete without Dirksen being a featured speaker—especially where the Republican women are concerned. He is their glamour boy, their patriot, their statesman, their inspiration and can give a rip roaring inspirational speech. He likes to address the ladies by beginning something like this: "Girls . . . I'm a little breathless this morning . . . who wouldn't be with all this loveliness and all this grace."

He once said, to thunderous applause, before a Republican women's group: ". . . an ancient lawgiver in Greece once observed: 'Greece rules the world, Athens rules Greece, I rule Athens, and my mother rules me.' He recognized womanpower even in those ancient days, and I recognize it today. I think Republican womanpower can be the greatest force in this Republic for the preservation of the heritage that we want to transmit.''

He entertains, flatters, cajoles, and makes the ladies feel as if each one is important to him and to the cause. Regardless of what he says, they always wish he would talk longer.

FAMOUS DIRKSENISMS

ANOTHER LOVELY LADY ADMIRER OF THE SENA-
TOR'S IS KIM NOVAK, WHO VISITED THE SENATOR
ON ONE OF HER TRIPS TO THE EAST. SHE IS A
NATIVE OF THE SENATOR'S HOME STATE.

6

FAMOUS DIRKSENISMS

■ Noted for his ability to hold an audience spell-bound with his tone, manner and innate sense of showmanship, Everett Dirksen is also well known for his unique expressions. Many have been repeated by newsmen, colleagues and audiences who respond to his rhetoric and we felt the book would be incomplete without including as many of these "Dirksenisms" as possible.

The flowery language and apparent ease with which Dirksen seems to pull magnificently sounding phrases out of the air are the sum and substance of his whole career and his long-standing romance with words. He loves them! To him words are living breathing symbols for him to use as a concert conductor uses fine musical instruments in developing a perfect symphony.

Filibuster has always been a rather offensive word to the Senator who brushes aside such an indelicate term by explaining it this way: "extended periods of expression which somehow made it difficult to secure action on a bill . . ."

*   *   *

He likes to originate his own metaphors and one of his oft-quoted ones is: "That idea has as much effect as a snowflake on the bosom of the Potomac."

*   *   *

Once wearying of a long Senate session as Christmas neared: "The sun has begun to shine through the old oaken door and the shadow of Santa is falling across the Senate floor."

*   *   *

ONE OF DIRKSEN'S GREAT ASSETS IS HIS ABILITY TO MAKE OTHERS SMILE AND HIS WIT APPARENTLY HAS MADE ITS TARGET WITH HOUSE MINORITY LEADER, GERALD R. FORD, MICHIGAN.

SENATOR DIRKSEN AT HIS WEEKLY PRESS CON-
FERENCE WITH GERALD R. FORD, GETS A POINT
ACROSS WITH ANOTHER WITTICISM AS HE TRIES
TO FIND OUT WHAT TO BELIEVE ABOUT THE DEM-
OCRATIC ADMINISTRATION — WHICH HE FRE-
QUENTLY CALLS ON THE CARPET.

The Golden Voice of The Senate

When he was campaigning in 1952 against the then-Democratic presidential candidate, Adlai Stevenson: "To elect Adlai Stevenson would be like leaving on the soiled diaper and merely changing the safety pin."

※   ※   ※

Upon campaigning against Senator Scott Lucas for his Senate seat in 1950, Dirksen made a strong appeal to his constituents: "Let's quit placing Marshall Plan mustard plasters on an economic ulcer that calls for the knife."

※   ※   ※

Upon winning his first election 1932: "The ambition to sit in Congress is probably similar to the flu . . . everybody gets it at some time or other. While it had been lurking in my system like some deadly virus, it did not become virulent until 1930."

※   ※   ※

Also in his comments on his 1932 campaign: "My esteemed Democratic opponent was beseeching the voters to give Mr. Roosevelt a Democratic Congress. And so, the Republican electorate marched to the polls on election day, as full of assurance as the little boy who whistles as he passes a cemetery after dark."

※   ※   ※

In summing up the Great Society in his year-end report to the Republican Party in 1966: "Under the Great Society a nation is beset by uncertainty, queasy doubts and bewilderment. Meanwhile the Administration goes its higgledy-piggledy way, its high priests no longer the flower of American culture who pursue domestic social progress with the pop-eyed ardor of a Harpo Marx chasing blondes.''

＊　　＊　　＊

When President Johnson was trying to pressure the Senator into some commitment on an Administration stand, he called Dirksen three days in a row searching for a definite answer. The first two times Senator Dirksen said he would ''think it over.'' The third time the President insisted on a definite answer. Dirksen replied, ''All right, I'll give you a definite 'maybe.'''

＊　　＊　　＊

When he was hospitalized in February, 1966, the Senator wrote some comments to be read by Thruston Morton (R. Ky.) about the tax-cut proposal then being discussed. Among his most amusing comments was: ''You can imagine my bed-ridden amazement, my pajama-ruffled consternation, yes, my pillow-laden astonishment this week, to learn that three Republican-sponsored proposals to assist in achieving laudable goals had been defeated by very narrow White House telephonic half-Nelsons known as the 'Texas Twist.'''

＊　　＊　　＊

Occasionally, when he wishes to express the fact that the Senate is not moving rapidly toward a conclusion: ''The Senate is the victim of a fortuity.''

＊　　＊　　＊

If a Senator speaks too much: "I shall invoke upon him every condign imprecation . . ."

*   *   *

He has cautioned fellow speakers in the manner of addressing an audience: "Never pound on the desk too hard; you may hurt yourself."

*   *   *

At a press conference following the breaking of his thighbone: "If I have to, I can use the crutches for weapons . . . The Bible says Samson slew the Philistines with a jawbone of an ass . . . I may have to slay an ass with the jawbone of a crutch."

*   *   *

Following the making of his record, "Gallant Men": "A great part of me has gone into that record. I think I would die unhappy unless I made some contribution to putting America, particularly young America, back into the stream of tradition."

*   *   *

Upon his seventieth birthday: "Timewise, I have reached the age of seventy; but ideawise or outlookwise, I'm still fifty or less. I haven't become reconciled to the calendar because I try to keep up with the times."

*   *   *

When he assumed his post as Minority Leader in 1959: "I've only got thirty-three soldiers, the Democrats have sixty-seven. That's why this administration has legislative indigestion."

*   *   *

FAMOUS DIRKSENISMS

SENATOR DIRKSEN'S "RIGHT ARM," HIS RECEP-
TIONIST-SECRETARY FOR MANY YEARS IN HIS MI-
NORITY LEADER OFFICE, GLEE COMIEN, ENJOYS A
RECORDING MADE FOR THE SENATOR BY RED
SKELTON. LOOKING ON FROM THE LEFT IS ARCH
LUSTBERG, EXECUTIVE WITH CHAPPELL MUSIC
CO., NEW YORK, WHO DIRECTED THE SENATOR IN
HIS RECORDING SESSIONS FOR CAPITOL RECORDS.
ON THE RIGHT IS BRIG. GENERAL JAMES D. HITTLE,
DIRECTOR OF NATIONAL SECURITY AND FOREIGN
AFFAIRS FOR VETERANS OF FOREIGN WARS.

In being questioned once about whether or not he ever deducted clothes as a political expense: "Not to be offensive, I came so close to it once. It was my first White House party and I had no long tails and no white tie. I was beside myself. I didn't know what to do. I finally went to the White House in a rented suit. As a result, when my constituents heard about this they collected $2,700. But I told them to divide it among the Salvation Army, Red Cross and others. At long last, I did not deduct from my income tax, although I could have felt justified in doing so because of embarrassment I went through. It was a matter of judgment."

      *   *   *

He is fond of closing a speech by saying: ". . . I think we ought to come to a termination here on a gently high and felicitous note."

      *   *   *

He likened the New Frontier to the clatter of dishes and fewness of victuals. He said that it was born at the Los Angeles Convention in July, 1960, where the Chairman broke twenty-four gavels, ". . . and that made a clatter in itself. There was a lot of applesauce with a dash of Hollywood, and plenty of confusion, and that's where the New Frontier was born. Then the candidates were selected—JFK-LBJ. And, of course, there was a keynote. I saw an interesting editorial after the keynote—

AT HIS PRESS CONFERENCES SENATOR DIRKSEN,
HERE WITH HIS HOUSE COUNTERPART, GERALD
R. FORD, MICHIGAN—GETS OFF SOME OF HIS BEST
"DIRKSENISMS." TO SENATOR DIRKSEN'S LEFT
STANDS JOHN FISCHER, COUNSEL TO THE MINOR-
ITY LEADER OF THE SENATE, ONE OF THE MOST
POPULAR MEN ON THE HILL AND AN ASTUTE
LEGISLATIVE ANALYST.

The Golden Voice of The Senate

SENATOR MARGARET CHASE SMITH (R. MAINE) PRESENTS SENATOR DIRKSEN WITH A BOUQUET OF MARIGOLD, THE FLOWER HE HAS BEEN TRYING TO HAVE NAMED AMERICA'S NATIONAL FLOWER FOR YEARS. HOWEVER, HE SEEMS TO BE ENJOYING THE AROMA OF THE ROSE HE IS SMELLING— ALSO ONE OF HIS FAVORITE FLOWERS. HE IS A GREAT LOVER OF AND GROWER OF FLOWERS AND GENERALLY BRINGS FLOWERS IN FROM HIS LITTLE PLACE IN VIRGINIA SO HE CAN HAVE THEM IN HIS OFFICE.

it was only one sentence. It said: 'And when he was done, he was done.' "

❊   ❊   ❊

He refers the twisting of figures by the Washington wizards to pull the wool over the eyes of the American public as ". . . hallucinatory estimates for masquerade and mirage in an extravaganza of political chicanery. . ."

In April, 1963 he described Washington in a speech about the New Frontier: ". . . Let me welcome you to your Capital, let me bid you welcome to the Federal City, let me bid you welcome to the Capital of the World . . . and to the financial center of the world . . . because it's to this city that all the countries of the world repair with their tin cups. This is the home of planned deficit. Deficits used to occur, but they were never planned . . . today they're planned. This is presently the home of confusion of the calculated type, this is the land of a hundred billion budgets, this is the laboratory where all things happen."

7

DOING WHAT COMES NATURALLY, DIRKSEN THE
PHILOSOPHER PLANTS SOME OF HIS FAVORITE
MARIGOLDS ON THE SENATE GROUNDS. KNOWING
HOW WELL DIRKSEN LIKES THE MARIGOLD AND
HOW MUCH HE WANTS IT TO BE THE NATIONAL
FLOWER, SENATORS HARRISON WILLIAMS, NEW
JERSEY, AND B. EVERETT JORDAN, NORTH CARO-
LINA, HAD A MARIGOLD PLANTING PARTY FOR
DIRKSEN, JULY 13, 1967.

DIRKSEN — PHILOSOPHER

■ I believe it most appropriate to delve into some of the philosophies that Senator Everett McKinley Dirksen espouses and to review what he considers the basic concepts by which man must live if he is to be worthy

An oft-told story is one which most appropriately mirrors his faith and philosophy. It begins when he was in the depths of despair and agony. His career had flowered magnificently since his election to the House of Representatives in 1932. He had enjoyed being the center of much attention and had become known for his brand of oratory and for his fearlessness in expressing his beliefs. For fifteen years he was center stage and in a spot he dearly loved. Tragedy struck in 1947, when he began to have trouble with his eyes.

For weeks he went through a series of elaborate tests: always the same devastating answer was given— no cure for an inflammation of the retina of his right eye, called chorioretinitis. Doctor after doctor recommended removal of the eye: to leave it, they reasoned, would mean that it might infect the left eye. A German specialist pronounced this case "cancer."

Not satisfied with any of the diagnoses, he went to Johns Hopkins Hospital for further consultations. There they, too, suggested surgery and soon.

"My wife and I talked this over for many days and prayed about this awful thing that had beset me," Dirksen related. "The agony of pain was too much at times and I spent hours talking with the Big Doctor Upstairs."

JUNIOR SPOKESMEN FOR CORN RE-
FINING VISIT WITH DIRKSEN TO GET
HIS LEGISLATIVE PHILOSOPHY ON
THE CORN PROBLEM. THEY ARE
FROM LEFT TO RIGHT: ELLIOTT
BURRILL YOUNG, TRIVOLI, ILLINOIS;
GERALD HOEWING, ARGYLE, IOWA;
AND CHARLES BRUNS, NEW LENOX,
ILLINOIS.

JOHN HECKER, A YOUNG ADMIRER
OF SENATOR DIRKSEN, GETS TO
DISCUSS SOME POLITICAL PHILOS-
OPHY WITH THE MINORITY LEADER
OF THE SENATE.

Finally, the Dirksens, in great sadness and despair boarded the train for Baltimore to have the Congressman submit to surgery. On the way, in his excruciating physical and mental misery, he once more dropped to his knees in the aisle of the train car. He said he asked God to help him to bear this trial and to guide him in coping with it. He also asked Him if blindness was to be his lot—the answer was "No!"

He reported to his doctor at Johns Hopkins, who urged him to hasten and prepare for surgery. Dirksen replied, "I guess I won't be going to surgery, because I found the answer before I came here."

Surprised and quizzical, the doctor asked, "Whom did you see?"

"Well, I called on the Big Doctor Upstairs—and the answer is 'No!'" He and his Louella turned and left the hospital.

But they still had a long way to go before the eye would be all right. They decided to give it a long rest and have more meditation with the Big Doctor. He resigned his seat in the House, which evoked from his colleagues a deluge of eulogies and urgings not to leave but to reduce his rigorous schedule in Congress. This, he said, he could not do, but must take care of his eyesight.

It was at this time when the late Sam Rayburn made his memorable comment—"If they are going to send Republicans to Congress, let them send Republicans of the Everett Dirksen kind."—most unusual thing for this noted Democratic legislator.

Dirksen returned to the Senate in 1951 with his eye fairly well recovered.

He calls the power of prayer, in which he has always believed, the mightiest force. "But," he adds, "you must be in constant touch."

It is no mystery, then, that he continues to push for prayer to be accepted in the schools. He has asked many an audience in his most sepulchral tones: "Is there anything more ennobling than prayer? A New York court forbade two young children to say in school: 'God is great, God is good, and we thank Him for this food.' What are we coming to?"

He cites many examples of schools across the country which have deleted the word *God*. On the Senate floor in September, 1966, he had a lengthy debate on the subject and in his comments he noted "Now, already, problems are developing with respect to the treatment of Christmas, Santa Claus, Christmas decorations, Christmas carols, the Nativity scene and everything pertinent to Christmas.

"In the suburban school district just outside Pittsburgh, where they planned to use the Nativity scene in a public school, they went down to see an attorney to get an opinion. Finally, his opinion was, 'Well, it will be all right if you present it in a cultural vein.'

"How in God's name do we present the manger in a cultural vein and have any significance left?

126

"How ludicrous, how stupid, how silly are they getting, those destroyers who want to destroy the religious traditions of this country?

"Interest is mounting in this matter of prayer in the public schools, and it will continue to mount. If I have anything to do with it, it will escalate and mount even faster. . . . It will not be stopped by the social engineers, by the world savers, by the cynics, or by some professors—that strange kind of liberal who is bemused by the idea of prayer in public schools, where pupils and students spend more of their waking hours than they do at home or in the church combined.

"In the various parts of the country, teachers are now asserting the right to eliminate from the *Pledge of Allegiance* the words 'under God.'

"On the basis of court decisions, a conscientious objector no longer need profess a religious belief in order to obtain deferment from military service. The suggestion has been made that as a substitute he offer evidence of membership in a pacifist organization.

"Efforts are underway in various quarters to end tax exemptions for religious institutions.

"The question has been raised concerning the propriety of having prayer aboard United States vessels.

"One school board felt that to have an invocation or a benediction at a graduation exercise came within the ban.

"Pupils in one Long Island school have refused

o join in the *Pledge of Allegiance* on the ground that
it has become meaningless by repetition.

"Flying a pennant over a municipal building in
New Jersey containing the words, 'One Nation Under
God,' has been regarded as open to legal attack.

"I think of the children, the millions whose souls
need the spiritual rehearsal of prayer.

"Right now we are in the football season. . . .
Imagine the Chicago Bears football team, made up of
green, inexperienced, unpracticed and unrehearsed
players, undertaking a game against the Cleveland
Browns. It would be unthinkable because they have
not been disciplined by practice. The soul needs practice too. It needs rehearsal. . .

"Prayer is a roadmap to God. It should become
the greatest adventure for young minds. Each must
find the way for himself. This takes some doing . . .
the development of right habits, the building of spiritual
muscle. This can come only from practice and rehearsal
day after day when young minds are alert.

"How strange we spend hundreds of millions of
public funds every year to develop physical fitness and
harden the muscles of American youth, but when it
comes to hardening the spiritual muscles through the
practice and rehearsal of prayer, it becomes enshrouded
in quaint legalism and the jargon of church and state.

"Mr. President, I finish by saying: Give Caesar
what he requires, but give God a little also."

It is no surprise, in the face of all the concern about the courts of the land ruling out any mention of the Divinity, to learn that Senator Dirksen's favorite hymn is "A Mighty Fortress is Our God," that one of his favorite books is the Bible. He quotes liberally from the Bible, especially St. Paul, Corinthians and the Psalms.

The Senator is equally as strong in his comments and his philosophies regarding the treatment around the world of our representatives, the flag and prestige and preeminence of the United States. He urges caution in becoming embroiled before we know all the circumstances, but believes in maintaining our strength. He noted once, "In many areas around the world, it appears that respect for us has vanished. I am not so naive as to believe that some far-off country will love us particularly and lavish affection on us for what we may do for it. I concluded long ago that probably the only thing we can get is respect; and that respect we will gain through strength. But we must be very sure that we are on good ground; that our facts are straight; and that we either know or do not know whether there was an element of provocation that can so easily call forth an equivalent expression, and use that as a basis for an interdiction by Congress in a piece of legislation that will have its repercussions in the chancelleries of the world.

"But arbitrary, capricious, and precipitate action

The Golden Voice of The Senate

THE LONG HOURS PUT IN BY SENATORS AT COM-
MITTEE HEARINGS ARE STAGGERING. HERE THE
SENATORS QUESTION WITNESSES AND PONDER
THE EVIDENCE. LEFT TO RIGHT: SENATOR PHILIP
A. HART, MICHIGAN; SENATOR CLIFFORD P. HAN-
SEN, WYOMING AND SENATOR DIRKSEN.

LORNE GREENE, THE FAMED BEN CARTWRIGHT
OF TV, GOT THE RED CARPET TREATMENT UPON
HIS VISIT TO WASHINGTON WHERE HE WAS EN-
TERTAINED BY THE MASTER SCENE STEALER,
SENATOR DIRKSEN.

will not further the cause of the United States as a leader of the free world. That leadership has been thrust upon us, and we could not avoid that responsibility even if we wanted to do so.''

Senator Dirksen frequently expounds his theories on the subject of how to handle situations, and particularly one's self—especially for the young who come to him for advice. He advises four points in dealing with almost any situation: 1. In a verbal slugfest, watch your temper, choose your words oh! so carefully; profane or insulting language can kill a glorious argument. 2. Learn to tell good stories. 3. Oppose with vigor, but never so vigorously that you lose a friend. 4. When dealing with people who differ, first determine how much common ground there is. Then try to close the gap.

He is a master at following his own advice, and tells the story about trying to get a plumber out to his house one evening to do some work on a broken washing machine. He said he spent about thirty minutes persuading the reluctant repairman to come. One of his listeners asked: "Why didn't you just tell him to snap to it?''

Dirksen pointed out: "I didn't just want him here. I wanted him in a good frame of mind, prepared to do an excellent job. *The oil can is mightier than the sword!''*

He considers a hardheaded attitude of solid opposition a destructive element: "If you follow a course
of solid opposition you can create a stalemate which
is not in the best interests of the country."

Opposition for the sake of stubborn opposition is
hardly the Senator's theory; opposition must be handled
in a constructive manner, tempered with consideration
of other points of view and new information relating
to the subject at hand. He always analyzes his attitudes,
evaluates his knowledge and listens with thoughtful
comprehension to another's side of the issue. He has
altered his direction as a result of this well-rounded,
open-minded approach, and for better results in most
instances.

He was asked by some journalists why he has, over
the years, changed his position or altered it on some
of the issues of the day. "Well, consistency is a hob-
goblin of small minds," he explained. "Was it Emer-
son who said it? I have often thought the only people
who do not change their minds are sleeping peacefully
in some cemetery or in an institution—involuntarily—
and have lost the capacity of changing their minds.
So, I hope the time will never come when I can't
adjust to new circumstances and new conditions, because it is an accelerated world."

Illustrating his philosophy on changing his point
of view, he related this anecdote: "Changing conditions
call for new evaluations and that may mean a change

in position. I sometimes think of the Johns Hopkins professor who had nailed down a thesis that he thought was quite durable and that could not be torn down. But his associate evaluated it and began pretty soon to tear it apart. In great agony the professor said: 'Is there nothing eternal?' His associate replied: 'Yes, one thing is eternal and that is change.' "

He recalls the message by Abraham Lincoln when he addressed Congress in 1862: "The dogmas of the quiet past are inadequate to the stormy present. The occasion is piled high with difficulty and we must rise with the occasion. As our case is now so we must think anew and act anew. . . . We must first disenthrall ourselves and then we shall save the country."

In saving the country his attention is forever directed toward the laws and regulations which nibble away our freedoms. Once he prepared a speech on "Frogs and Freedom." In it he pointed out that "You put a frog in a kettle of cold water and let him sit on the bottom and turn on the gas, and you'll have him cooked. But if you heat the water first, and drop the frog in, his reflexes are so fast, he pops right out of the kettle. Now you know, that is the way freedom is lost. Put freedom in the bottom of the kettle and boil it away, a little at the time, and bring the temperature up, and when you're ready to retrieve it, you can't because freedom is dead. So think sometime about frogs and freedom."

He likens this free government to "an old water-logged scow. It doesn't move very fast, it doesn't move very far at one time, but it never sinks and maybe that is the reason we have a free government today. I was thinking how many free governments are just in too great a hurry that suddenly flop over and take on a dictatorial and despotic cast because they can't wait for normal forces to undertake the changes that are necessary in the constant climb of people to a better life."

Throughout his philosophy runs a strong thread of patriotism filled with poetry. His feeling and love of poetry are an integral part of his being, and while it is difficult for him to point to a certain poem as his favorite, he appears to lean in the direction of "Invictus," by William Ernest Henley, Kilmer's "Trees," Seegar's "In Flanders' Fields," and Whittier's "Snowbound." Recently another has been added to his long list of best-loved poems: it was a dedication to him by the Poet Laureate of Maryland, Vincent Godfrey Burns, and appeared in *The Evening Capital* of Annapolis, Maryland, March 23, 1968. With the poet's permission we present it here. The poet did not name it, but we will:

EVERETT DIRKSEN: THE STATESMAN

A gallant man with shock of curly hair—
A doleful voice, compassionate and kind—
A sorrowful face, most deeply lined with care,
Reflecting giant problems on his mind!

A wisdom born of suffering and pain—
A warm good humor and gracious smile—
A gay indifference to gold or gain
And patience, without bitterness or guile!

Thank God for men of high integrity
Who will not stoop to slander or to smear,
Who serve their God and country faithfully,
As enemies mass their Red battalions here;
Inspired by our noble heritage
He leads a new crusade for freedom in our
    age!

BEMUSED, HE STUDIES THE OIL PAINTING OF HIM-
SELF.

OFFICIAL BIOGRAPHY OF
EVERETT MCKINLEY DIRKSEN

■ *Everett McKinley Dirksen was born January 4, 1896, at Pekin, Illinois, in the heart of the state. His middle name, McKinley, derives from the martyred President. He attended Pekin High School and the University of Minnesota Law School, married Louella Carver of Pekin and they have one daughter, Mrs. Howard H. Baker, Jr.*

He began his military service in World War I as an enlisted man but rose from private to corporal, to sergeant and then was commissioned in the field as a 2nd Lieutenant. He served seventeen months overseas with the 328th Field Artillery, the 19th Balloon Company and the Second Section of the General Staff.

Back in civilian life he became a dredging and drainage contractor, engaged in the manufacture of electric washing machines, was co-proprietor of a wholesale bakery, a director of the American Savings and Loan Association at Pekin, is an attorney, a member of the Illinois Bar Association and the District of Columbia Bar Association.

He entered public service when elected Commissioner of Finance of the city of Pekin in 1926 and served four years. As a candidate for Congress in 1930 he was defeated in the primary.

In 1932 he was nominated and elected to Congress, serving eight consecutive terms from the 73rd through the 80th Congresses. He retired voluntarily from Congress on

SENATOR AND MRS. DIRKSEN WITH THEIR GRAND-
SON, DAREK DIRKSEN BAKER, ATTEND THE TEN-
NIS MATCHES BETWEEN THE YOUNGER REPUB-
LICANS AND DEMOCRATS.

The Golden Voice of The Senate

SENATORS EDWARD W. BROOKE, MASSACHUSETTS,
AND EVERETT SALTONSTALL, MASSACHUSETTS,
SWAP QUIPS WITH DIRKSEN.

January 3, 1949. In 1950 he was prevailed upon to become a candidate for the United States Senate and was elected on November 7, 1950, over the Honorable Scott W. Lucas, the Senate Majority Leader; renominated for the Senate in April 1956; re-elected November 6 for a second term; re-elected to a third Senate term on November 6, 1962.

Senator Dirksen's party service has included membership on the Republican National Congressional Committee, 1938 to 1946, vice chairman, 1938 to 1946; delegate to the Republican Policy Conference at Mackinac Island in 1943; and delegate to the Republican National Convention in 1940, and all subsequent conventions. In 1944 he was formally endorsed by more than forty members of the House of Representatives for a place on the Republican National Ticket. Served as chairman of the Republican Senatorial Campaign Committee from 1951 through 1954. He served as Minority Whip for the 85th Congress and was selected as Minority Leader for the 86th, 87th, 88th, 89th, and 90th Congresses.

His Committee service in Congress has included the Committees on Territories, Immigration and Naturalization, Banking and Currency, Select Committee to Reorganize the Executive Branch, Select Committee on Real Estate Bondholders Reorganization, Select Committee on Air Safety, Joint Committee on Appropriations, and Committee on Legislative Budget. During the 80th Congress, he served as chairman of the Committee on the District of Columbia and as chairman of the Subcommittee on Agricultural Appropriations. He was also designated as chairman of a Joint House Committee to survey conditions in Europe. He is presently serving on the Judiciary and Finance Committees of the Senate. In addition he is Chairman of the Subcommittee on Federal Charters, Holidays and Celebrations of the Senate Judiciary Committee; a member of the Special Committee on Aging and the Republican Policy Committee.

Among other organizations, Senator Dirksen is a member of the American Legion, the Veterans of Foreign Wars, Masons-Shriners, Elks, Eagles, Oddfellows, Moose, Izaak Walton League, Illinois Bar Association, and American Bar Association.

In the last few years Senator Dirksen has been honored with Honorary degrees from a number of institutions. He received the degree of Doctor of Laws from Hope College at Holland, Michigan, Bradley University at Peoria, Illinois, Depaul University at Chicago and Lincoln Memorial University at Harrogate, Tennessee.

ACKNOWLEDGMENTS

■ Our thanks to the following for their assistance in collecting material and stories for this book:

Senator Mike Mansfield, *Senate Majority Leader (D., Mont.)*

Francis R. Valeo, *Secretary of the Senate*

Senator Howard H. Baker, Jr., *Son-in-law of Senator Dirksen (R., Tenn.)*

John R. Fisher, *Consultant to the Republican Leadership*

Congressman Albert W. Watson *(R., S.C.)*

Mrs. Glee Gomien, *Secretary to the Senator and often called his "right arm."*

Mrs. Sarah Van, *Secretary to Mr. Fisher*

Mrs. Frances Appel, *A Secretary to the Senator*

Edgar H. Miller, *Press Aide to Senator Baker*

Robert Parker, *Maitre de of the Senate Dining Room*

Charles W. Steadman, *Chairman of the Board and President, Steadman Security Corporation*

Ben Regan, *Partner, Hornblower & Weeks-Hemphill, Noyes, and Commissioner of the New York Port Authority*

Brigadier General J. D. Hittle *(Ret., U. S. Marines)*, *Director of National Security and Foreign Affairs for Veterans of Foreign Wars*

Vincent Godfrey Burns, *Noted Author and Poet Laureate of Maryland*

Dr. Ronald Stinnett, *Former Aide to the Vice President and Noted Political Analyst, President, The Washington Group, Inc., Business and Political Consultants*

RESOURCE MATERIAL

The Congressional Record • Leading newspapers and magazines • The pictures given through the courtesy of the Senator's office were taken by the GOP Senate Photographic staff now manned by Arthur Scott and F. Clyde Wilkinson with the exception of Shields News Photographers, the City News Bureau (both in Washington, D.C.) and The Waltrex Studio of Mattoon, Ill.

THE ACROPOLIS BOOKS
CONGRESSIONAL LEADERSHIP SERIES

■ Following the publication of the first volume of this series, Mr. Donald G. Tacheron, Associate Director of the American Political Science Association said:

"With few exceptions, the leaders of Congress have escaped the attention of serious biographers. Such works are sorely needed by the student of politics who is concerned with the functions of Congressional Leadership and the vital role it plays in our governmental system. This monograph on the Acting President pro tempore of the Senate is a step in the right direction. . . ."

■ It is planned that eventually all leadership positions in the Congress will be covered with individual volumes of the Acropolis Books Congressional Leadership Series. Several additional volumes are already projected.

So far, the following have been published:

Vol. No. 1: The Acting President pro tempore of the Senate— HOW A SENATOR MAKES GOVERNMENT WORK (METCALF OF MONTANA by Richard D. Warden with Foreword by Senator Paul Douglas) $4.50 (*cloth only*)

Vol. No. 2: Liberal Leader in the House (THOMPSON OF NEW JERSEY by Augusta Elliott Wilson with Foreword by Senator Edward M. Kennedy) $4.50 (*cloth*); $2.75 (*paper*)

Vol. No. 3: The Minority Leader of the Senate—THE GOLDEN VOICE OF THE SENATE (DIRKSEN OF ILLINOIS by Annette Culler Penney with Foreword by Senator Mike Mansfield) $4.95 (*cloth*); $2.75 (*paper*)

Available at your bookseller, or directly from the publisher
ACROPOLIS BOOKS/ Colortone Building, 2400 17th St., N.W., Washington, D.C. 20009